# I CHING INVESTING:
# THE SECRET TO
# MAKING MONEY IN THE
# STOCK MARKET

## NITIN ACH

# I CHING INVESTING: THE SECRET TO MAKING MONEY IN THE STOCK MARKET

# Contents

## The I Ching Stock Indicator

*"If I have seen farther, it is by standing on the*

*shoulder of giants."*

*— Sir Isaac Newton*

Imagine having an all-encompassing indicator that can revolutionize your stock trading game. Can you picture it? Well, let me take you on a journey through a hypothetical conversation I had with my trader buddy, whom I affectionately call Skeptic.

"Hey, Skeptic!" I hollered excitedly, "You've got to check out this groundbreaking stock indicator I've developed."

Skeptic shot me a dubious look, his skepticism written all over his face. "Are you for real?" he retorted, "Aren't there already a gazillion stock indicators out there? Is this just another one of those 'get rich quick' schemes?"

I fired back, "Come on, Skeptic! Keep an open mind. Hear me out before you pass judgment."

"Alright, spill the beans," he conceded.

I leaned in and asked, "Wouldn't it be amazing to have an indicator that does it all?" I grinned,

"Introducing the I Ching Stock Indicator, my friend. This isn't your run-of-the-mill indicator. It's a game-changer. It's like having a trusted companion guiding you through the wilds of the Stock Market."

Skeptic burst into laughter, "LOL!"

I continued, "You see, most technical indicators rely on patterns that have already been spotted and acted upon by other traders. Everyone interprets these patterns differently."

Skeptic nodded vigorously, "You're preaching to the choir."

I went on, "Some traders see past price patterns and assume history will repeat itself. They buy, while others see an overbought market and start short-selling. It's a real maze."

Skeptic chimed in, "Tell me about it. It's frustrating when you've done your homework and your stock suddenly nosedives."

I agreed, "Exactly. The stock market is a complex beast, more art than science. When a bunch of traders all interpret the same pattern the same way, that's when technical indicators work."

Skeptic leaned in, curious, "So, how does your indicator solve this puzzle? And what's the deal with this I Ching stuff?"

I explained, "The I Ching is one of the world's oldest and eerily accurate divination systems. It centers on 'Change' and time's role in shaping our world. Stock prices, too, change with time as market participants interpret various situations affecting listed companies."

Skeptic leaned closer, intrigued, "Go on."

I continued, "The I Ching Stock Indicator taps into this. It offers 64 patterns or hexagrams to decode the hidden messages in stock prices. It tells which sectors will show more movement during the period under review. It will help you take an informed decision. It's your edge."

Skeptic's eyes widened, "Wow! So, will I always be right if I use your method?"

I cautioned, "Never get too cocky in trading. Even the best methods can't guarantee 100% success. Emotions play a big role. Great traders stay cool no matter what."

I added, "Don't solely rely on the I Ching Stock Indicator.

Consult your broker and analyze price charts. And remember, a single day's reading won't predict a stock's future. Back-test to get a clearer picture."

Skeptic was now genuinely interested, "Hmm. You've got my attention. I'll give it a shot. Thanks!"

Follow the wisdom of the I Ching Stock Indicator, but remember, success in the stock market demands discipline and a well-rounded approach to trading.

Happy trading, folks!

**A Final Word:** This work is currently in progress, and it will continue to evolve and improve over time. As the project develops, new features, functionalities, and content will be added to enhance the overall experience. You can expect regular updates and improvements as the work moves towards completion.

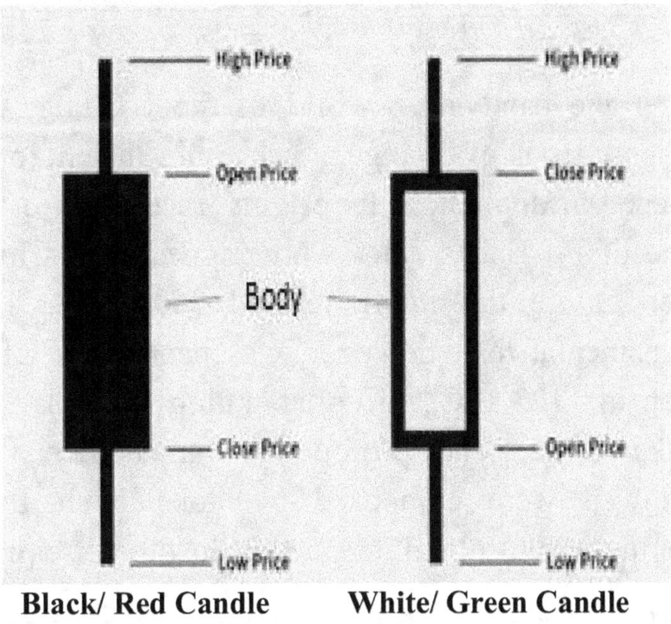


**Black/ Red Candle**    **White/ Green Candle**

**Japanese Candlesticks**

Enter the captivating world of the I Ching, the Chinese Book of Change, a venerable ancient tome steeped in divination. Its origins trace back to the time of Fu Hsi, a ruler who reigned over China eons before the flood, around 3000 B.C. The fundamental text, however, was penned by King Wen in 1123 B.C., in collaboration with his son Duke Chou. The profound commentaries that followed were composed by none other than Confucius himself, alongside his devoted disciples.

This isn't just any old divination system; it's one of the planet's most ancient and enduring systems. For thousands of years, across dynasties and eras, from emperors to everyday folks, millions have turned to the I Ching for guidance and reaped its wisdom. And now, you're about to embark on your own journey with it. Imagine it as your ever-present, sagacious companion, standing by your side, always ready to offer sage advice whenever you seek it. The fact that it's still thriving today speaks volumes about its enduring relevance.

The I Ching places "Change" at the very heart of its observations, recognizing **time** as an essential element in the structure of the world and the development of humanity. Remarkably, the stock market follows a similar pattern, relying on the ever-shifting sands of time. As market participants interpret incoming information, stock prices ebb and flow throughout the trading day. The stock market, you see, digests all available data, and this is mirrored in its prices—but often only for the information available at that very moment.

Now, the stock market isn't always the most dependable place. Sometimes, a company's performance has seemingly no bearing on its stock price. In this realm, rumors and false information run rampant, posing a minefield for newcomers. It's a scary prospect that keeps many at bay.

However, to succeed in the stock market, you need an edge—a unique advantage that sets you apart from the rest. Without it, no amount of discipline or financial acumen can save you from potential disaster. Enter the I Ching Stock Indicator, your ultimate secret weapon. It's your guide, telling you when to invest or trade, when to enter the market, which sectors to dive in, and crucially, when to stand aside. There will be times when its counsel clashes with your intuition, but in hindsight, you'll often find it was precisely what the circumstances demanded.

This book is for everyone; it's tailored for beginners, intermediates, and even advanced traders. For algorithmic traders, it's a powerful tool capable of performing wonders. Think of it as a lifelong companion, a seer, and a mentor.

So, have faith in the timeless principles contained within these pages. Trust in the wisdom of the oracle and let it guide your path. Your endeavors in the stock market will be richly rewarded. And if ever you doubt its guidance, simply compare it to the unfolding market conditions.

In the beginning, consider paper trading to hone your skills without risking your capital. Conduct backtesting, build your confidence, and then, when you're ready, consult the I Ching Stock Indicator during your actual trading endeavors.

**Your financial journey is about to take an exciting, transformative turn.**

## Some Important Topics

Before we delve into the topic of I Ching investing, I'd like to discuss some key subjects that will be covered in our readings.

These topics include:

- Sector Analysis

- Guidance for Algorithmic Traders

- Proper Money Management While Dealing in Stocks

- Utilizing the Kelly Criterion for Sound Money Management

- Unlocking the Enigma of the Reward/Risk Quotient

- Implementing Stop Loss Orders

- Understanding Support and Resistance Levels

Now, let's explore each of these topics in more detail to provide you with a comprehensive understanding of I Ching investing and its various components.

## How Important is Sector Analysis for the Investor or Trader?

In the fast-paced world of finance, where markets can fluctuate in the blink of an eye, the role of sector analysis cannot be understated. Whether you're an investor looking to build a long-term portfolio or a trader seeking short-term gains, understanding the nuances of sector analysis can significantly impact your success. In this article, we'll delve into the importance of sector analysis for both investors and traders, exploring its role in decision-making, risk management, and overall profitability.

## Introduction:

Sector analysis involves evaluating and understanding specific industry segments within the financial markets. It goes beyond individual stocks or assets and assesses how different sectors of the economy are performing. This analysis plays a pivotal role in guiding investment and trading decisions, providing valuable insights into market trends and potential opportunities.

**What is Sector Analysis?**

Sector analysis is the process of examining various sectors of the economy, such as technology, healthcare, or energy, to identify trends, opportunities, and risks associated with each. It involves studying the financial health, growth prospects, and competitive landscape of companies within a particular sector.

**Why is Sector Analysis Important?**

For investors, sector analysis is essential for diversifying their portfolio. By spreading investments across multiple sectors, they can reduce the risk associated with having all their assets in one basket. If one sector experiences a downturn, investments in other sectors can offset potential losses.

- **Identifying Growth Opportunities:**

Sector analysis helps investors identify sectors with high growth potential. For instance, the technology sector has seen substantial growth in recent years, making it an attractive option for those seeking long-term capital appreciation.

- **Portfolio Optimization:**

Investors can optimize their portfolios by strategically allocating resources to sectors that align with their financial goals and risk tolerance. This approach ensures a balanced and resilient portfolio.

- **Trader's Perspective:**

Traders benefit from sector analysis by identifying sectors that are likely to outperform in the short term. By focusing on sectors with positive momentum, traders can capitalize on price fluctuations and generate quick profits.

- **Timing Market Swings:**

Sector analysis helps traders anticipate market trends and shifts. By staying ahead of the curve, they can make informed decisions on when to enter or exit positions, maximizing their gains.

**Tools and Techniques for Sector Analysis:**

There are several methods for conducting sector analysis, each offering unique insights:

- **Fundamental Analysis:**

Fundamental analysis involves assessing a sector's financial health by examining factors such as revenue, earnings, and market share. This approach helps investors and traders identify undervalued or overvalued sectors.

- **Technical Analysis:**

Technical analysis relies on historical price and volume data to predict future price movements. Traders use charts and technical indicators to make decisions based on market trends.

- **Sentiment Analysis:**

Sentiment analysis involves gauging market sentiment through news, social media, and other sources. It helps investors and traders understand market psychology and sentiment-driven price movements.

- **I Ching Analysis:**

This is a novel concept that I've delved into within this book. The I Ching can provide insights into sectors that may have demonstrated potential shifts over the past seven periods, as well as make educated guesses about sectors likely to be active in the upcoming period. This unique approach offers valuable assistance to investors and traders, enabling them to pinpoint sectors that might be either undervalued or overvalued.

**Challenges in Sector Analysis:**

While sector analysis can be highly beneficial, it comes with its share of challenges:

- **Market Volatility:**

Sectors can be highly volatile, and sudden market shifts can catch investors and traders off guard. It's essential to stay updated and adapt to changing market conditions.

- **Information Overload:**

The abundance of data and information available can be overwhelming. Investors and traders must filter through the noise to focus on relevant insights.

**FAQs**

**1. Is sector analysis relevant for all types of investors**

Sector analysis is relevant for both individual and institutional investors. It can be adapted to suit various investment strategies.

## 2. How often should I update my sector analysis?

The frequency of updates depends on your investment horizon. Long- term investors may review sector analysis less frequently than short-term traders.

## 3. Can sector analysis help in predicting market crashes?

While sector analysis can provide warning signs, predicting market crashes with certainty is challenging.

## 4. Should I completely rely on the I Ching for sectoral analysis, or is it better to view it as a guiding tool for making decisions?

When it comes to using the I Ching for sectoral analysis, it's important to approach it with a balanced perspective. The I Ching can be a valuable guide for decision-making, offering insights and potential trends based on its symbolism and interpretations. However, it is not infallible and should not be relied upon solely.

Consider using the I Ching as one tool among many in your decision-making process. Combine its guidance with thorough research, market analysis, and your own judgment. This way, you can harness the wisdom it offers while maintaining a realistic understanding of its limitations.

Ultimately, trust in the I Ching should be tempered with a critical and informed approach to ensure well-rounded decision-making in the realm of sectoral analysis.

## 5. What role does sector analysis play in a diversified investment portfolio?

Sector analysis is instrumental in achieving diversification by helping investors allocate assets across different sectors to manage risk effectively.

## 6. What are the titles of sectors and their respective subcategories for companies that are publicly traded on prominent stock exchanges?

Sure, take a look at this. It's a thorough compilation of the 11 sectors and their corresponding subcategories for companies listed on well-known stock exchanges.

## 1. Energy:

- Oil and gas exploration and production
- Oil and gas refining and marketing
- Utilities
- Renewable energy
- Solar energy
- Wind energy
- Hydroelectric power
- Geothermal energy
- Biomass energy
- Coal
- Nuclear power

## 2. Materials:

- Metals and mining
- Iron and steel
- Aluminum
- Copper
- Nickel
- Zinc
- Lead
- Gold
- Silver
- Platinum

- Chemicals and materials
- Industrial chemicals
- Specialty chemicals
- Plastics and rubber
- Construction materials
- Glass and ceramics

## 3. Industrials:

- Aerospace and defense
- Aircraft and parts
- Missiles and defense systems
- Spacecraft and parts
- Machinery and equipment
- Heavy machinery
- Construction equipment
- Farm equipment
- Food processing equipment
- Industrial automation
- Transportation
- Automobiles and parts
- Trucks and buses
- Railroads
- Airlines
- Shipping
- Water transportation
- Construction
- General contractors
- Specialty contractors
- Building materials suppliers

## 4. Utilities:

- Electric utilities
- Natural gas utilities
- Water utilities
- Waste management

## 5. Healthcare:

- Pharmaceuticals
- Biotechnology
- Medical devices
- Healthcare services
- Hospitals
- Clinics
- Health insurance

## 6. Financials:

- Banks
- Commercial banks
- Investment banks
- Savings and loans
- Insurance
- Life insurance
- Property and casualty insurance
- Health insurance
- Investment services
- Asset management

- Brokerage firms
- Mutual funds

## 7. Consumer Discretionary:

- Automobiles
- Luxury cars
- Mass- /Red/Black Candlemarket cars
- Truck and SUV manufacturers
- Consumer electronics
- TVs
- Computers
- Smartphones
- Audio and video equipment
- Clothing and accessories
- Apparel
- Footwear
- Jewelry
- Food and beverage
- Restaurants
- Food retailers
- Beverage companies
- Retailing
- Department stores
- Specialty retailers
- Online retailers
- Travel and leisure
- Airlines
- Hotels
- Cruise lines

- Theme parks

## 8. Consumer Staples:

- Food and staples retailing
- Grocery stores
- Convenience stores
- Foodservice companies
- Household products
- Personal care products
- Household cleaning products
- Durable goods
- Personal products
- Cosmetics
- Toiletries
- Razors and blades

## 9. Information Technology:

- Hardware
- Semiconductors
- Computer hardware
- Networking equipment
- Software
- Software publishers
- IT services
- Cloud computing
- IT services
- Business process outsourcing

- IT consulting
- Systems integration
- Telecommunications
- Wireless carriers
- Cable and satellite TV providers
- Telecom equipment manufacturers

## 10. Communication Services:

- Media and entertainment
- Broadcasting
- Cable and satellite TV
- Film and television studios
- Video game publishers
- Telecommunications services
- Wireless carriers
- Cable and satellite TV providers
- Telecom equipment manufacturers

## 11. Real Estate:

- Real estate investment trusts (REITs)
- Residential REITs
- Commercial REITs
- Industrial REITs
- Office REITs
- Retail REITs
- Property management
- Construction

**In Conclusion:**

Sector analysis is a critical tool for both investors and traders. It provides valuable insights into market dynamics, risk management, and profit potential. By understanding the nuances of sector analysis and applying the right techniques, individuals can make more informed financial decisions and enhance their overall success in the world of finance.

Remember to conduct your sector analysis diligently and adapt your strategies as market conditions evolve. The financial landscape is dynamic, and sector analysis can serve as your compass in navigating the ever-changing waters of finance.

Hey, algo traders, here's an intriguing challenge for you!

How about putting the periodicity of sixty-four unique patterns to the test across various time-frames—daily, weekly, and monthly?

Delve deeply into the data to uncover hidden insights:

- How frequently did a specific stock or index exhibit a particular pattern during the timeframe under examination?
- What were the gains and losses associated with each pattern if you bought a stock or index the day, week, or month after the pattern occurred?
- What were the gains and losses associated with each pattern if you shorted a stock or index the day, week, or month after the pattern occurred?
- What was the average profit or loss for each trade executed?
- Which strategy (buying or shorting) resulted in the most profitable outcomes?
- Which timeframe led to the most profitable results?
- What was the ratio of wins to losses?

- Can you identify the highest profit and the greatest loss?
- And, of course, be sure to pinpoint the maximum drawdown.
- Is the advice given by "The I Ching Says" sensible?
- I used three methods to draw the candlestick patterns: the Close Price Method, the Pivot Point Method, and the Open and Close Japanese candlesticks method. Which method was the most accurate in predicting the market?

Now, the real question is,

- Which of these patterns exhibit a statistical edge?
- Are there any hidden gems among them?
- Count them up—how many of these patterns hold the key to unlocking trading success?

This exciting journey into pattern analysis promises to unveil valuable insights for traders looking to gain a competitive edge in the market. It could be a reliable path to significant wealth in the stock market.

**Words of Advice, blah, blah:**

An algorithmic trader, or algo-trader, should conduct a thorough and meticulous backtesting process to evaluate the effectiveness and viability of a trading system. Backtesting is a critical step in trading system development and involves testing a strategy or algorithm using historical market data.

Here are the key elements an algo-trader should check while backtesting a trading system:

## 1. Historical Data Quality:

Ensure that the historical data used for backtesting is accurate, reliable, and reflects real market conditions. Any inaccuracies or gaps in data can lead to flawed results.

## 2. Data Timeframe:

Select an appropriate timeframe for your data, whether it's tick-by-tick data, minute data, hourly data, daily data, or any other interval relevant to your trading strategy.

### 3. Data Sourcing:

Choose a reputable source for your historical data. Many trading platforms and data providers offer historical data for various assets and markets.

### 4. Trading Costs:

Factor in trading costs such as commissions, spreads, and slippage when simulating trades. These costs can significantly impact the profitability of a trading strategy.

### 5. Strategy Parameters:

Clearly define the parameters of your trading strategy, including entry and exit rules, risk management criteria, and position sizing rules.

### 6. Market Conditions:

Be mindful of different market conditions, including bull markets, bear markets, and ranging markets. Test your strategy under various conditions to assess its adaptability.

### 7. Overfitting and Curve Fitting:

Guard against overfitting, where a strategy is tailored too closely to historical data and performs poorly in live trading. Avoid curve fitting by keeping your strategy as simple and robust as possible.

## 8. Out-of-Sample Testing:

After optimizing your strategy using historical data, validate its performance on unseen data, often referred to as out-of-sample testing. This helps determine if the strategy is robust and not just tailored to historical patterns.

## 9. Risk Management:

Implement sound risk management techniques, such as setting stop-loss orders and position sizing based on risk tolerance. Assess how the strategy handles drawdowns and adverse market conditions.

## 10. Portfolio Diversification:

If you're trading a portfolio of assets, consider how your trading system allocates capital among different assets or positions. Diversification can reduce risk.

### 11. Slippage and Liquidity:

Account for slippage, which occurs when the execution price differs from the expected price due to market volatility. Test how your strategy performs in illiquid markets.

### 12. Market Impact:

Evaluate the impact of your trades on the market, especially for large positions. Large orders can move prices, affecting your strategy's performance.

### 13. Backtesting Software:

Use reliable backtesting software or platforms that can accurately simulate trades and provide detailed performance metrics.

### 14. Realistic Expectations:

Maintain realistic expectations about the performance of your trading system. Not all strategies will be profitable, and losses are a part of trading.

## 15. Continuous Monitoring and Optimization:

Recognize that markets evolve over time. Regularly monitor and update your trading system to adapt to changing market dynamics.

## 16. Psychological Factors:

Consider the psychological aspects of trading, such as discipline and emotional control. Backtesting can provide insights into how well you can stick to your strategy during drawdowns or losing streaks.

## 17. Conclusion:

By thoroughly examining these factors during the backtesting process, algo-traders can gain a better understanding of their trading systems' strengths and weaknesses, ultimately improving their chances of success in live trading.

# Proper Money Management While Dealing in Stocks

In the fast-paced world of stock trading, one thing is certain: Proper money management is the cornerstone of success. We understand that navigating the intricate landscape of the stock market can be a daunting task, especially for those new to the game. That's why we're here to guide you through the essential principles of managing your finances wisely while dealing in stocks.

**The Importance of Money Management:**

Before we delve into the nitty-gritty details of effective money management in stock trading, let's address why it's so crucial. Imagine your finances are a ship, and the stock market is the unpredictable sea. Without a sturdy rudder and a capable captain, your ship may get lost in the stormy waters. Money management serves as that rudder, steering your financial vessel to safety and profitability.

**Setting Realistic Goals ;**

One of the first steps in proper money management when dealing in stocks is setting realistic financial goals. It's essential to have a clear vision of what you want to achieve. Are you looking for short-term gains, or are you in it for the long haul? Define your objectives, whether they involve wealth accumulation, retirement planning, or funding a specific life goal.

**Diversification of Investments:**

Diversification is a term that frequently circulates in the world of finance, and for good reason. Spreading your investments across different asset classes and industries helps reduce the risk associated with stock trading. By diversifying, you can mitigate the impact of a downturn in a particular sector while potentially benefiting from the upswing in another. This strategy acts as a safety net for your investments.

**Risk Assessment:**

Understanding and managing risk is a cornerstone of successful stock trading. Every investment carries some level of risk, and it's vital to assess the risks associated with your portfolio.

Conduct thorough research on the stocks you plan to invest in. Consider factors such as market volatility, company financials, and industry trends. This in-depth analysis will enable you to make informed decisions that align with your risk tolerance.

**Position Sizing:**

Once you've evaluated the risks, it's time to determine the appropriate size for each position in your portfolio. This process, known as position sizing, ensures that you don't overcommit your capital to a single investment. A common rule of thumb is to limit each position to a certain percentage of your total portfolio. This way, even if one stock takes a hit, your overall financial ship remains steady.

**The Role of Stop-Loss Orders:**

In the turbulent waters of stock trading, even the most seasoned investors encounter rough seas. To protect your investments, consider implementing stop-loss orders. These orders automatically sell a stock when it reaches a predetermined price, limiting potential losses. They act as your financial lifebuoy, ensuring that a sudden market crash doesn't sink your portfolio.

**Monitoring and Adjustment:**

The stock market is dynamic, with prices fluctuating constantly. Effective money management requires continuous monitoring of your portfolio. Regularly assess the performance of your investments and make adjustments as needed. If a stock no longer aligns with your financial goals or exhibits concerning signs, don't hesitate to cut ties and reallocate your resources.

**The Importance of Patience:**

Patience is a virtue, especially in the world of stock trading. It's essential to resist the urge to make impulsive decisions based on short-term market fluctuations. Stick to your well-thought-out investment plan, and remember that wealth accumulation through stocks is often a long-term endeavor.

**Seek Professional Advice:**

While we've provided you with valuable insights into proper money management in stock trading, it's crucial to acknowledge that the stock market can be complex and unpredictable. If you're unsure about your investment decisions or need personalized guidance, consider seeking advice from a certified financial advisor. Their expertise can help you navigate the market with confidence.

**In Conclusion:**

In the ever-evolving world of stock trading, proper money management remains a beacon of hope and stability. By setting realistic goals, diversifying your investments, assessing risks, implementing stop-loss orders, and monitoring your portfolio, you can navigate the stock market's waters with confidence. Remember, patience is key, and seeking professional advice when needed can be a wise move.

In the previous chapter, we explored the significance of diversifying investments. Although diversification is important, it could be simpler to say than to achieve. How much cash should we invest in each stock? How soon do we purchase or sell those stocks? By designing a money management system, all of these queries can be resolved.

In this chapter, we'll examine the Kelly Criterion, one of the many methods you may use to manage your money well.

**The Background**:

The Kelly Criterion was initially created by John Kelly, a former employee of AT&T's Bell Laboratory, to help the company with problems related to long-distance telephone signal noise. The gambling industry, however, quickly learned about the technique and recognised its potential as an ideal betting system once it was published as "A New Interpretation Of Information Rate" (1956).

**The Kelly Criterion has two fundamental parts:**

- Win probability - The likelihood that any particular deal you make will result in a profit.
- Win/loss ratio: The sum of all profitable trades divided by the sum of all losing trades.

Then, Kelly's equation is adjusted to include these two variables:

$$W - [(1 - W) / R] = Kelly\%$$

Where:

W = Chance of winning

R is the win-loss ratio.

**Making Use of It :**

These easy steps can be used to implement Kelly's system:

1. Review your most recent 50–60 deals. Simply calling your broker or looking up your most recent tax returns (provided you declared all of your trades) will allow you to find out. If you're an experienced trader with a well-developed trading strategy, you can just do a back test on the strategy and use the findings. However, the Kelly

Criterion makes the assumption that you will trade in the same manner as in the past.

2. Determine the likelihood of winning ("W"). To do this, divide the total number of trades (positive and negative) by the number of trades that returned a positive amount. The closer it is to one, the better this number is. Any value over 0.50 is desirable.

3. Determine "R," or the win-to-loss ratio. Divide the average gain of the winning transactions by the average loss of the losing trades to achieve this. If your average gains are higher than your average losses, you should have a number greater than 1. As long as the number of losing trades stays low, a result less than one is workable.

4. Enter the following data into Kelly's formula: $K\% = W - [(1 - W) / R]$.

5. Note the Kelly proportion that the formula produces.

**Understanding the Outcomes:**

The magnitude of the positions you ought to be taking is represented by the percentage (a value less than one) that the equation yields. As an illustration, if the Kelly percentage is 0.05, you should own 5% of each equity. In essence, this approach tells you how much diversification is appropriate.

However, the system does call for some common sense. No more than 20 to 25 percent of your capital should be allocated to one equity, regardless of what the Kelly percentage suggests. Any more than this entails significantly more risk than the majority of people ought to accept.

# Unlocking the Enigma of the Reward/Risk Quotient

In the realm of trading, there exists a pivotal metric known as the reward-risk ratio (RRR), an intricate gauge instrumental in assessing the potential profitability of a trade vis-a-vis its prospective losses. In essence, this ratio quantifies the anticipated returns in relation to the level of risk assumed. Calculated by dividing potential gains by potential losses, a lofty reward-risk ratio heralds an advantageous trading prospect, while a meager ratio implies the converse. However, the reward-risk ratio encompasses a multitude of facets that extend far beyond this elementary understanding.

## Deciphering the Reward-Risk Ratio:

The process of computing the reward-risk ratio is by no means labyrinthine. To illustrate, consider a trader evaluating a prospective short trade proposition with an entry price at 16387.8, a Stop Loss set at 16565.8, and a Take Profit price of 15854.6. The journey to discerning the reward-risk ratio follows a straightforward path:

1. Begin by quantifying the risk, defined as the interval between the entry price and the Stop Loss:

Risk = Stop Loss – Entry price = 16565.8 – 16387.8 = 178.0

2. Subsequently, calculate the potential reward of the trade, characterized as the span from the Entry price to the Take Profit:

Reward: Entry price – Take Profit = 16387.8 – 15854.6 = 533.2

3. The reward-risk ratio materializes as the division of the reward by the earlier computed risk:

Reward-risk ratio = Reward / Risk = 533.2 / 178.0 = 2.99 = 3

Frequently, you'll encounter the reward-risk ratio represented as 3:1, signifying that the trade promises threefold rewards in comparison to the associated risks.

For long (buy) trades, the methodology remains consistent. If you employ Tradingview, their Long/Short Position tool effortlessly automates the calculation of your reward-risk ratio, obviating the need for manual computation.

**Insights Unveiled by the Reward-Risk Ratio:**

Ideally, a trader scrutinizes the reward-risk ratio prior to embarking on a trade, thereby evaluating its profitability and verifying that it offers a commensurate reward potential.

Let's delve into two pivotal aspects to grasp this better.

**1. Reward-Risk Ratio and Trade Profitability:**

In the context of our previous trade example sporting a 3:1 reward-risk ratio, it's conceivable that, by replicating the same trade conditions consistently, you could sustain three losses and still break even, provided you secure one profitable trade out of every four:

- Trade 1 – Loss: Incurs a 178-point loss (cumulative loss of 178)

- Trade 2 – Loss: Incurs a 178-point loss (cumulative loss of 356)

- Trade 3 – Loss: Incurs a 178-point loss (cumulative loss of 534)

- Trade 4 – Win: Yields a profit of 533.2 points

**- Total Outcome:** Approximately breakeven (± 0 points)

This underscores the significance of engaging in trades offering a substantial reward-risk ratio. It dispels the notion that a trader must emerge victorious in all, or even a majority, of their trades to realize long-term gains. If a trader can secure victory in two out of every four trades, maintaining the same 3:1 reward-risk ratio, they'll conclude the day with a profit.

## 2. Assessing Trade Reward Potential:

Before committing to a trade, it behooves the trader to dissect the chart's landscape and appraise the trade's potential reward. In scenarios where the price must surmount formidable support or resistance levels en route to the Take Profit threshold, the trade's reward potential could be constrained.

Ideally, traders should identify opportunities where price traverses without encountering significant support or resistance barriers en route to the desired target. The greater the number of price "hurdles" obstructing the path from entry to target, the likelier it becomes that price fluctuations will impede progress, thwarting the attainment of the ultimate objective.

**The Reward-Risk Ratio and Your Winrate:**

I alluded earlier to the interplay between the reward-risk ratio and a trading system's winrate. With a 3:1 reward-risk ratio, a trader can afford to lose three out of four trades and still conclude without financial loss. For a 3:1 reward-risk ratio, the minimum requisite winrate to break even is 25%, derived by dividing 1 by 4, indicating one successful trade for every four attempts.

Naturally, the higher the reward-risk ratio, the lower the winrate needed to achieve breakeven.

The following table elucidates the winrate prerequisites for achieving breakeven at varying reward-risk ratios:

| Reward-to-risk ratio | Winrate required / Breakeven point |
|---|---|
| 1:1 | 50% |
| 2:1 | 33% |
| 3:1 | 25% |
| 4:1 | 20% |
| 5:1 | 17% |

**The Pitfalls of an Elevated Reward-Risk Ratio:**

Many traders may surmise that targeting a high reward-risk ratio should simplify the path to profits, as it necessitates a lower winrate. While this notion holds theoretical validity, it is not without caveats.

To attain a lofty reward-risk ratio, a trader can either position their target levels at a considerable distance from the entry price to augment the trade's potential reward or utilize stop loss orders in close proximity to the entry to mitigate risk exposure. Both strategies yield a higher reward-risk ratio. However, what implications does this bear for the trade, and why isn't bigger necessarily better in the realm of the reward-risk ratio?

A broad trade target implies that the price trajectory necessitates extended periods to reach its destination. Additionally, the farther the target veers from the entry, the slimmer the likelihood of full realization. The wider the target, the lower the probability of the price achieving the ultimate goal. Wider targets, therefore, present greater challenges and often culminate in diminished winrates.

Conversely, a closer stop loss heightens the susceptibility of the price triggering the stop loss. Even minor price oscillations and subdued volatility can trigger stop losses when a tight stop loss order is employed. The proximity of the stop loss translates into a reduced winrate, as it becomes easier for the price to trigger the stop loss.

**Mastering the Interplay Between Stop Loss and Take Profit:**

Understanding the inherent relationship between the distances of stop loss and take profit levels can empower traders to make judicious decisions and enhance their risk management prowess. Many budding traders remain oblivious to how adjustments in stop loss or take profit orders can dramatically impact trading performance and fundamentally reshape the complexion of their trades.

**The Quest for the Optimal Reward-Risk Ratio:**

Regrettably, there exists no one-size-fits-all solution to ascertain the optimal reward-risk ratio. Novice traders often gravitate towards a trend-following approach that typically demands a substantial reward-risk ratio—a challenging feat. As elucidated, a higher reward-risk ratio generally corresponds to a lower winrate and prolonged trade duration. Both factors can pose formidable obstacles for novice traders, potentially prompting them to prematurely exit profitable trades, thereby forfeiting substantial gains.

For those embarking on their trading journey, it is advisable to commence with a more modest reward-risk ratio. Such a strategy typically yields a higher winrate and facilitates the swift cultivation of confidence, courtesy of more frequent victories.

In the previous chapter, we discussed the use of stop-loss in our trading strategies. Here, we will explore the concept of stop-loss and its prudent application.

In the world of investing, risk management is a crucial aspect that can often make the difference between success and failure. One essential tool that investors use to protect their capital and minimize losses is the stop-loss order. Stop-loss orders come in various forms, each serving a specific purpose and catering to different trading strategies.

In this comprehensive guide, we'll explore the various types of stop-loss orders and how they can be effectively employed to safeguard your investments.

**Introduction:**

Before diving into the specifics of different stop-loss orders, let's first understand what a stop-loss order is and why it's essential in trading. A stop-loss order is an order placed with a broker to buy or sell a security once it reaches a specific price level. The primary purpose of a stop-loss order is to limit potential losses by automatically triggering a trade when the market moves against the investor's position.

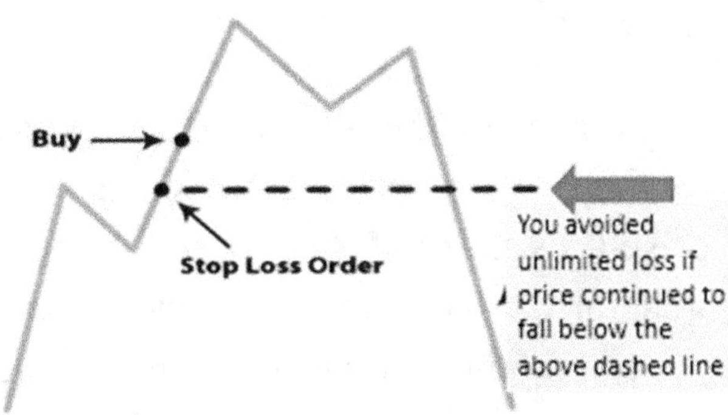



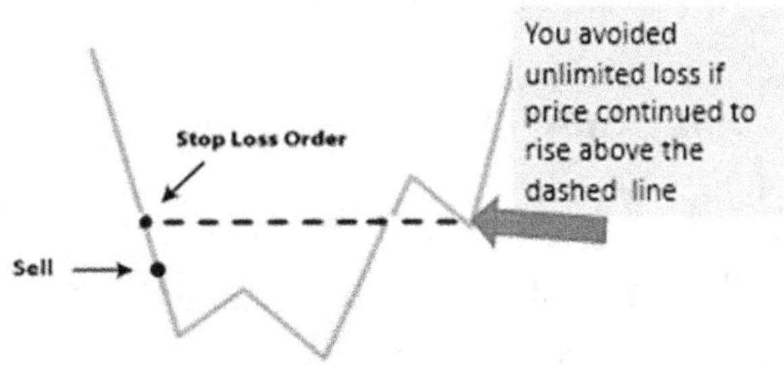



**The various types of stop-loss orders are:**

## 1. Market Orders:

Market orders are the simplest form of stop-loss orders. When a market order is triggered, it executes the trade at the current market price. While market orders guarantee execution, they may not guarantee a specific price, and in highly volatile markets, the actual execution price may differ significantly from the stop price.

## 2. Limit Orders:

Limit orders, on the other hand, allow investors to specify the exact price at which they want to buy or sell a security. If the market price reaches the predefined limit price, the order is executed. This type of stop-loss order provides more control over the execution price but doesn't guarantee execution if the market doesn't reach the limit price.

## 3. Trailing Stop Orders:

Trailing stop orders are dynamic and adjust with the market's movement. They are set as a percentage or dollar amount away from the market price, and as the market price increases, the trailing stop price follows, always maintaining the preset distance. If the market reverses and reaches the trailing stop price, the order is triggered.

### 4. Stop-Limit Orders:

Stop-limit orders combine features of both stop and limit orders. They have two price levels: the stop price and the limit price. When the market reaches the stop price, a limit order is placed at the limit price. If the market doesn't reach the limit price, the order remains unexecuted.

### 5. Volatility Stop Orders:

Volatility stop orders take into account market volatility. They adjust the stop price based on the security's price fluctuations. In times of high volatility, the stop price widens, while it tightens during periods of low volatility.

### 6. Percentage Stop Orders:

Percentage stop orders are based on a fixed percentage drop from the entry price. This type of stop-loss order is popular among traders as it adapts to the security's price and volatility.

### 7. Time Stop Orders:

Time stop orders are set for a specific duration. If a trade doesn't reach its target within the allotted time, the order is canceled. This type of stop-loss is useful for traders who want to limit the time their capital is tied up in a trade.

## 8. Contingent Orders:

Contingent orders are linked to other events in the market. For example, a trader might place a stop-loss order contingent on the release of a specific economic report or news event.

## 9. Guaranteed Stop Orders:

Guaranteed stop orders provide an absolute level of protection. They guarantee execution at the specified stop price, regardless of market conditions. However, they often come with higher fees.

## 10. Hidden Stop Orders:

Hidden stop orders are not visible to other market participants. They are often used by institutional traders who want to keep their trading strategies confidential.

## How to Choose the Right Stop-Loss Order:

Selecting the right stop-loss order depends on your trading strategy, risk tolerance, and market conditions. It's essential to understand the strengths and weaknesses of each type and choose the one that aligns best with your goals.

**Common Mistakes to Avoid:**

While stop-loss orders can be powerful risk management tools, they are not without pitfalls. Common mistakes include setting stop-loss orders too close to the entry price, neglecting to adjust stop-loss levels as market conditions change, and using excessive leverage.

**Benefits of Using Stop-Loss Orders:**

The benefits of using stop-loss orders are numerous. They protect your capital, help you stick to your trading plan, and reduce emotional decision-making. Additionally, they allow you to exit losing trades gracefully.

**In Conclusion:**

Stop-loss orders are indispensable tools for any trader or investor looking to manage risk effectively. Understanding the various types of stop-loss orders and when to use them is crucial for success in the financial markets. By incorporating these strategies into your trading plan, you can navigate the markets with confidence.

## Understanding Support and Resistance Levels in Stock and Index Trading

In the world of stock and index trading, success often hinges on a deep comprehension of various technical analysis tools and strategies.

One of the most critical concepts that traders, both novice and experienced, should grasp is the significance of support and resistance levels. These key price levels serve as crucial indicators in making informed trading decisions.

In this chapter, we will delve into the world of support and resistance levels, shedding light on their importance and how they can be effectively utilized to optimize your trading strategy.

**Defining Support and Resistance Levels:**

Support and resistance levels are foundational elements of technical analysis used by traders to identify potential price reversal points in the market. They are represented by specific price levels at which a stock or index tends to stop and change direction. Understanding these levels is paramount for traders seeking to make well-informed decisions.

# SUPPORT AND RESISTANCE

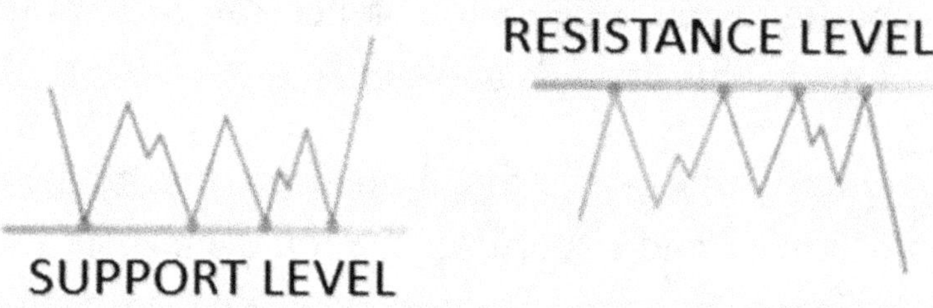



## Support Levels:

Support levels are the price points at which a stock or index tends to find buying interest, preventing it from falling further. Picture this as a safety net that prevents the price from plummeting. Traders often view support levels as ideal entry points for buying because they anticipate a bounce-back in prices from these levels. This is where demand for the asset typically outweighs the supply.

## Resistance Levels:

On the flip side, resistance levels are price points at which a stock or index faces selling pressure, preventing it from rising higher. Think of these levels as a price ceiling that the asset struggles to break through. Traders tend to see resistance levels as strategic points to consider selling their positions because they expect a pullback in prices.

## The Importance of Support and Resistance Levels:

Now that we've defined support and resistance levels, let's explore why they are of paramount importance to traders.

### 1. Decision-Making:

Support and resistance levels act as guideposts for traders when making crucial decisions. These levels help traders determine entry and exit points for their positions. For instance, if a stock reaches a well-established support level, it might be an opportune moment to buy, anticipating a price rebound. Conversely, when a stock approaches a strong resistance level, it may be wise to consider selling or taking profits.

### 2. Risk Management:

Effective risk management is fundamental to trading success. Support and resistance levels aid in defining stop-loss orders. By placing stop-loss orders just below a support level when buying or just above a resistance level when selling, traders can limit potential losses.

## 3. Market Psychology:

Support and resistance levels are not merely mathematical constructs; they also reflect market psychology. When a stock approaches a support level and bounces back, it signifies renewed buying interest and positive sentiment. Conversely, when a stock fails to breach a resistance level, it reflects selling pressure and caution among traders.

## Identifying Support and Resistance Levels:

The key to utilizing support and resistance levels effectively is the ability to identify them accurately.

Here are some methods and tips to help you in this endeavor:

## 1. Historical Data Analysis:

Reviewing historical price charts is a primary method for identifying support and resistance levels. Look for price levels where the stock or index has reversed direction multiple times in the past. These are likely significant support or resistance levels.

## 2. Round Numbers and Psychological Levels:

Round numbers, such as $50 or $100, often act as psychological support or resistance levels. Traders tend to pay close attention to these levels, making them more likely to hold.

## 3. Moving Averages:

Moving averages, both simple and exponential, can also help identify support and resistance levels. When the price moves close to or crosses a moving average, it can serve as a dynamic support or resistance level.

## 4. Volume Analysis:

Consider analyzing trading volumes alongside price movements. Significant price reversals often occur on high trading volumes, indicating strong support or resistance levels.

## In Conclusion:

Support and resistance levels are invaluable tools in the arsenal of any trader. They provide critical insights into potential price reversals, guide decision-making, and help manage risks effectively. By mastering the art of identifying and interpreting these levels, you can significantly enhance your trading strategy and increase your chances of success in the dynamic world of stock and index trading.

Remember, trading involves inherent risks, and no strategy is foolproof. It's essential to combine support and resistance analysis with other technical and fundamental analysis tools to make well-rounded trading decisions.

Alright, we've covered a lot of theory in trading. Now, let's get into the practical side of things.

Let's delve into the setup.

**1. Choose Your Price:** Start by picking a price for a stock or index. It can be the closing price or something called the Pivot Point (an average of the High, Low, and Close prices). You can also use Japanese candlestick patterns to help with this. Once you decide, stick with it.

**2. Select Time Interval:** Decide how often you want to track price changes. Daily changes are a good choice, but you can also try weekly, monthly, or yearly periods to see which one works best for you.

**3. Analyzing Price Trends:** To gain insights into price movements, examine seven consecutive days for daily tracking, seven consecutive weeks for weekly analysis, and apply a similar approach for monthly intervals.

**4. Labeling Prices:** The latest price is called P6, and the oldest one is labeled as P1. The prices in between are named P2, P3, P4, and P5. Additionally, you'll need a price just before P1, which we'll call P0, to analyze the price movement of P1.

**5. Price Patterns:** If the most recent price is higher than the preceding one **OR** if the closing price is greater than the opening price, we'll refer to it as a "+/Green/White Candle" pattern.

Conversely, if the latest price is lower than the one before it **OR** if the opening price is greater than the closing price, we'll call it a "-/Red/Black Candle" pattern.

**6. Action Lookup:** Please refer to the table below to locate the Action Number for your stock or index based on the patterns you have identified.

**7. Make Decisions:** Read the predictions based on the Action Number under **'The I Ching Says'** and utilize them as guidance for your investment decisions.

# Action Lookup Table

| Upper → / Lower ↓ | + + + | - - + | - + - | + - - | - - - | + + - | + - + | - + + |
|---|---|---|---|---|---|---|---|---|
| + + + | 1 | 34 | 5 | 26 | 11 | 9 | 14 | 43 |
| - - + | 25 | 51 | 3 | 27 | 24 | 42 | 21 | 17 |
| - + - | 6 | 40 | 29 | 4 | 7 | 59 | 64 | 47 |
| + - - | 33 | 62 | 39 | 52 | 15 | 53 | 56 | 31 |
| - - - | 12 | 16 | 8 | 23 | 2 | 20 | 35 | 45 |
| + + - | 44 | 32 | 48 | 18 | 46 | 57 | 50 | 28 |
| + - + | 13 | 55 | 63 | 22 | 36 | 37 | 30 | 49 |
| - + + | 10 | 54 | 60 | 41 | 19 | 61 | 38 | 58 |

Find the upper half of your Action at the top ($\rightarrow$) and the lower half on the left ($\downarrow$) and follow the row and column to where they intersect. That will be the number of your Action.

**Examples:**

**1. Close Price Method:**

Check out the stock prices for the period May 5, 2016 to May 13, 2016. Let us denote P0, P1, P2, P3, P4, P5 and P6 as the close prices of the stock on these dates.

| Date | Open | High | Low | Close | Price | Action | |
|---|---|---|---|---|---|---|---|
| May 13, 2016 | 22.5 | 22.92 | 22.5 | 21.18 | P6 | P6>P5 | ✚ |
| May 12, 2016 | 23.18 | 23.19 | 22.37 | 21.13 | P5 | P5<P4 | ▬ |
| May 11, 2016 | 23.37 | 23.39 | 23.11 | 21.64 | P4 | P4<P3 | ▬ |
| May 10, 2016 | 23.33 | 23.39 | 23.03 | 21.85 | P3 | P3>P2 | ✚ |
| May 09, 2016 | 23.25 | 23.44 | 23.15 | 21.71 | P2 | P2>P1 | ✚ |
| May 06, 2016 | 23.34 | 23.36 | 22.96 | 21.69 | P1 | P1<P0 | ▬ |
| May 05, 2016 | 23.5 | 23.52 | 23.17 | 21.81 | P0 | Pattern 18 | |

As per the Action Lookup Table, the **stock pattern is 18**.

## 2. Pivot Point Method:

Check out the stock prices for the period May 19, 2016 to May 27, 2016. Let P0, P1, P2, P3, P4, P5 and P6 be the average daily (Pivot) prices (High + Low + Close divided by3) of the stock.

| Date | Open | High | Low | Close | Pivot | Price | Action | |
|---|---|---|---|---|---|---|---|---|
| May 27, 2016 | 715 | 716.60 | 711.10 | 712.24 | 713.31 | P6 | P6>P5 | + |
| May 26, 2016 | 708.33 | 715.00 | 707.29 | 714.91 | 712.40 | P5 | P5>P4 | + |
| May 25, 2016 | 708 | 710.86 | 705.52 | 708.35 | 708.24 | P4 | P4>P3 | + |
| May 24, 2016 | 698.01 | 707.50 | 698 | 704.20 | 703.23 | P3 | P3>P2 | + |
| May 23, 2016 | 704.25 | 706.00 | 696.42 | 696.75 | 699.72 | P2 | P2<P1 | - |
| May 20, 2016 | 701.05 | 707.24 | 700 | 702.80 | 703.35 | P1 | P1>P0 | + |
| May 19, 2016 | 691.88 | 699.40 | 689.56 | 698.52 | 695.83 | P0 | Pattern 13 | |

As per the Action Lookup Table, the **stock pattern is 13**.

## 3. Open and Close / Japanese candlesticks method:

I won't delve into the intricacies of Japanese candlestick theory or create charts to demonstrate this technique. I assume you're already familiar with candlesticks. If you're not, you can find plenty of information about Japanese candlesticks on the internet. Please refrain from using this method with Heiken Ashi or other candlestick variations. Stick to regular candlesticks for this approach.

Now, let's examine the six consecutive opening and closing prices, along with the corresponding candlestick patterns for a hypothetical stock, starting from March 4 and concluding on March 11, 2016.

| Date | Open | Close | Candle | |
| --- | --- | --- | --- | --- |
| 11/03/2016 | 699.4 | 699.6 | Green | + |
| 10/03/2016 | 700.3 | 668.06 | Red | - |
| 09/03/2016 | 608.18 | 673.58 | Green | + |
| 06/03/2016 | 600.55 | 563 | Red | - |
| 05/03/2016 | 626.06 | 597.95 | Red | - |
| 04/03/2016 | 655.8 | 621.44 | Red | - |
| | | | Pattern 35 | |

The candles for March 11 and 9 would be Green/White, indicating that the closing prices were higher than the opening prices on those days.

Similarly, since the closing prices were lower than the opening prices, you would find Red/Black candles on March 10, 6, 5, and 4.

You should label the Green/White candles as "+/Green/White Candle" and the Red/Black candles as "-/Red/Black Candle." Arrange the candles in chronological order, as shown above, and consult the Pattern Lookup Table to find the corresponding pattern number.

As per the Action Lookup Table, the **stock pattern is 35**.

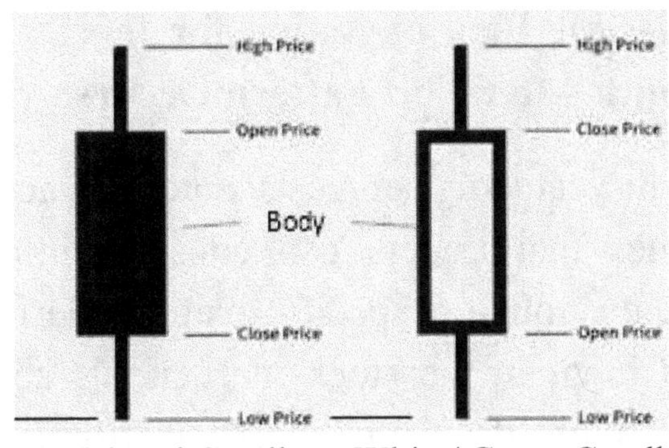


Black/ Red Candle    White/ Green Candle

**JAPANESE CANDLESTICKS**

**What do the following three categories mean?**

1a. Possible Plan of Action for the Day, Week, or Month After This Pattern Occurs:

1b. Check out these Sectors:

2. Likely Plan of Action for the Day Two, Week Two, or Month Two After This Pattern Occurs:

Let me provide a simplified explanation of these three categories:

## 1a. Possible Plan of Action for the Day, Week, or Month After This Pattern Occurs:

This category suggests potential actions and strategies that traders can consider immediately after they notice a specific pattern, derived from the I Ching, in the stock market. It's about what traders might do in the short term (day, week, or month) right after they spot this pattern.

For example, if the pattern indicates a positive trend for the next day, week, or month, traders might think about buying certain stocks, setting stop-loss orders, or making changes to their portfolio to align with this positive outlook.

## 1b. Check out these Sectors:

This category advises traders to pay attention to specific sectors within the stock market. Different sectors can perform differently based on various factors like economic conditions and market trends. When a particular pattern is observed, it may have a more significant impact on certain sectors.

For instance, if your analysis suggests that a particular pattern is favorable for technology stocks, you might recommend that traders focus their attention on the technology sector. This guidance helps traders target their investments more effectively.

## 2. Likely Plan of Action for the Day Two, Week Two, or Month Two After This Pattern Occurs:

This category deals with actions and strategies that traders should think about implementing a bit later, beyond the immediate reaction to the observed pattern. It's about planning for what might happen in the market in the slightly longer term—on the second day, second week, or second month after noticing the pattern.

In essence, these three categories provide traders with guidance on how to respond to specific patterns in the stock market. The first category is for immediate actions, the second category directs attention to relevant sectors, and the third category focuses on the immediate next period (day, week, month) planning based on the observed pattern.

# THE 64 PRICE PATTERNS AND THEIR INTERPRETATIONS

# Action 1

| Date | Price | Action | Sign/ Candle |
|---|---|---|---|
| End Date D6 | P6 | P6>P5 | +/Green/White Candle |
| D5 | P5 | P5>P4 | +/Green/White Candle |
| D4 | P4 | P4>P3 | +/Green/White Candle |
| D3 | P3 | P3>P2 | +/Green/White Candle |
| D2 | P2 | P2>P1 | +/Green/White Candle |
| D1 | P1 | P1>P0 | +/Green/White Candle |
| Start Date D0 | P0 | | |

**The I Ching Says:**

**1a. Possible Plan of Action for the Day, Week, or Month After This Pattern Occurs:**

"What goes up will come down. This is known as the 'reversion to the mean' theory. This pattern works best with daily candlesticks. Once the highest candle is formed, place a sell order below the low of this candle. Set an exit target and a trailing stop loss."

## 1b. Check out these Sectors:

Consumer Discretionary, Financial Services, Industrials.

## 2: Likely Plan of Action for the Day Two, Week Two, or Month Two After This Pattern Occurs:

There's a 50-50 chance that one of these two outcomes will happen:

"What goes up will come down. This is known as the 'reversion to the mean' theory. This pattern works best with daily candlesticks. Once the highest candle is formed, place a sell order below the low of this candle. Set an exit target and a trailing stop loss."

### OR

"Prepare for price swings and trade with proper money management."

| Date | Price | Action | Sign/ Candle |
|---|---|---|---|
| End Date D6 | P6 | P6<P5 | - /Red/Black Candle |
| D5 | P5 | P5<P4 | - /Red/Black Candle |
| D4 | P4 | P4<P3 | - /Red/Black Candle |
| D3 | P3 | P3<P2 | - /Red/Black Candle |
| D2 | P2 | P2<P1 | - /Red/Black Candle |
| D1 | P1 | P1<P0 | - /Red/Black Candle |
| Start Date D0 | P0 | | |

**The I Ching Says:**

**1a. Possible Plan of Action for the Day, Week, or Month After This Pattern Occurs:**

"What goes down will come up. This is known as the 'reversion to the mean' theory. This pattern works best with daily candlesticks. Once the lowest candle is formed, place a buy order above the high of this candle. Set an exit target and a trailing stop loss."

**1b. Check out these Sectors:**

Consumer Discretionary, Healthcare, Materials, Real Estate.

**2. Likely Plan of Action for the Day Two, Week Two, or Month Two After This Pattern Occurs:**

There's a 50-50 chance that one of these two outcomes will happen:

"What goes down will come up. This is known as the 'reversion to the mean' theory. This pattern works best with daily candlesticks. Once the lowest candle is formed, place a buy order above the high of this candle. Set an exit target and a trailing stop loss."

**OR**

"Exercise caution and anticipate a correction period ahead."

# Action 3

| Date | Price | Action | Sign/ Candle |
| --- | --- | --- | --- |
| End Date D6 | P6 | P6<P5 | - /Red/Black Candle |
| D5 | P5 | P5>P4 | +/Green/White Candle |
| D4 | P4 | P4<P3 | - /Red/Black Candle |
| D3 | P3 | P3<P2 | - /Red/Black Candle |
| D2 | P2 | P2<P1 | - /Red/Black Candle |
| D1 | P1 | P1>P0 | +/Green/White Candle |
| Start Date D0 | P0 | | |

**The I Ching Says:**

**1a. Possible Plan of Action for the Day, Week, or Month After This Pattern Occurs:**

"Maintain your current position. Expect initial resistance followed by success. Patience is necessary."

**1b. Check out these Sectors:**

Consumer Discretionary, Energy, Healthcare, Industrials, Materials, Real Estate, Technology, Telecommunication Services.

**2. Likely Plan of Action for the Day Two, Week Two, or Month Two After This Pattern Occurs:**

There's a 50-50 chance that one of these two outcomes will happen:

"You will have three opportunities to profit with this stock or index."

**OR**

"Defense and Real Estate stocks have a higher probability of success."

# Action 4

| Date | Price | Action | Sign/ Candle |
| --- | --- | --- | --- |
| End Date D6 | P6 | P6>P5 | +/Green/White Candle |
| D5 | P5 | P5<P4 | - /Red/Black Candle |
| D4 | P4 | P4<P3 | - /Red/Black Candle |
| D3 | P3 | P3<P2 | - /Red/Black Candle |
| D2 | P2 | P2>P1 | +/Green/White Candle |
| D1 | P1 | P1<P0 | - /Red/Black Candle |
| Start Date D0 | P0 | | |

**The I Ching Says:**

**1a. Possible Plan of Action for the Day, Week, or Month After This Pattern Occurs:**

"Stocks may experience a gap up or down, leading to price volatility. Carefully monitor the situation for an opportunity before making a move. This can lead to profitable outcomes."

**1b. Check out these Sectors:**

Consumer Discretionary, Consumer Staples, Energy, Healthcare, Industrials, Materials, Real Estate.

**2. Likely Plan of Action for the Day Two, Week Two, or Month Two After This Pattern Occurs:**

There's a 50-50 chance that one of these two outcomes will happen:

"If your stock is above or below the 200-period moving average, near or crossing 52-week highs, or nearing 52-week lows, or if its support/resistance levels have been breached, then consider it."

**OR**

"Maintain your current position. Expect initial resistance followed by success. Patience is necessary."

## Action 5

| Date | Price | Action | Sign/ Candle |
|---|---|---|---|
| End Date D6 | P6 | P6<P5 | - /Red/Black Candle |
| D5 | P5 | P5>P4 | +/Green/White Candle |
| D4 | P4 | P4<P3 | - /Red/Black Candle |
| D3 | P3 | P3>P2 | +/Green/White Candle |
| D2 | P2 | P2>P1 | +/Green/White Candle |
| D1 | P1 | P1>P0 | +/Green/White Candle |
| Start Date D0 | P0 | | |

**The I Ching Says:**

**1a. Possible Plan of Action for the Day, Week, or Month After This Pattern Occurs:**

"Avoid taking immediate action. Observe the stock's trend. Wait for the candle to close above the resistance level or below the support level before taking any action."

**1b. Check out these Sectors:**

Consumer Discretionary, Energy, Financial Services, Healthcare, Industrials, Materials.

**2. Likely Plan of Action for the Day Two, Week Two, or Month Two After This Pattern Occurs:**

There's a 50-50 chance that one of these two outcomes will happen:

"This stock is suitable for scalping."

**OR**

"If your stock is from the Consumer Discretionary sector and is currently trending, there's a probable chance of loss."

# Action 6

| Date | Price | Action | Sign/ Candle |
|---|---|---|---|
| End Date D6 | P6 | P6>P5 | +/Green/White Candle |
| D5 | P5 | P5>P4 | +/Green/White Candle |
| D4 | P4 | P4>P3 | +/Green/White Candle |
| D3 | P3 | P3<P2 | - /Red/Black Candle |
| D2 | P2 | P2>P1 | +/Green/White Candle |
| D1 | P1 | P1<P0 | - /Red/Black Candle |
| Start Date D0 | P0 | | |

**The I Ching Says:**

**1a. Possible Plan of Action for the Day, Week, or Month After This Pattern Occurs:**

"Entering the market incorrectly carries a high probability of loss. Seek advice from a market professional."

**1b. Check out these Sectors:**

Consumer Discretionary, Energy, Financial Services, Healthcare, Industrials, Materials.

## 2. Likely Plan of Action for the Day Two, Week Two, or Month Two After This Pattern Occurs:

There's a 50-50 chance that one of these two outcomes will happen:

"If a previously 'weak' stock suddenly gains attention, trading it can lead to success. For other stock categories or indices, check whether they are above or below the 200-period moving average, near or crossing 52-week highs, or nearing 52-week lows, or if their support/resistance levels have been breached."

### OR

"Anticipate small profits, but only at the end of the timeframe period."

# Action 7

| Date | Price | Action | Sign/ Candle |
| --- | --- | --- | --- |
| End Date D6 | P6 | P6<P5 | - /Red/Black Candle |
| D5 | P5 | P5<P4 | - /Red/Black Candle |
| D4 | P4 | P4<P3 | - /Red/Black Candle |
| D3 | P3 | P3<P2 | - /Red/Black Candle |
| D2 | P2 | P2>P1 | +/Green/White Candle |
| D1 | P1 | P1<P0 | - /Red/Black Candle |
| Start Date D0 | P0 | | |

**The I Ching Says:**

**1a. Possible Plan of Action for the Day, Week, or Month After This Pattern Occurs:**

"Selecting a leading stock in an active sector can yield profits, but patience is required."

**1b. Check out these Sectors:**

Consumer Discretionary, Energy, Healthcare, Industrials, Materials, Real Estate.

**2. Likely Plan of Action for the Day Two, Week Two, or Month Two After This Pattern Occurs:**

There's a 50-50 chance that one of these two outcomes will happen:

"If your stock is a market leader, there's a probable chance of success."

**OR**

"Buy with a small exit target in mind."

# Action 8

| Date | Price | Action | Sign/ Candle |
|---|---|---|---|
| End Date D6 | P6 | P6<P5 | - /Red/Black Candle |
| D5 | P5 | P5>P4 | +/Green/White Candle |
| D4 | P4 | P4<P3 | - /Red/Black Candle |
| D3 | P3 | P3<P2 | - /Red/Black Candle |
| D2 | P2 | P2<P1 | - /Red/Black Candle |
| D1 | P1 | P1<P0 | - /Red/Black Candle |
| Start Date D0 | P0 | | |

**The I Ching Says:**

**1a. Possible Plan of Action for the Day, Week, or Month After This Pattern Occurs:**

"Trade stocks that are trending, have gaps up or down, and avoid laggards."

**1b. Check out these Sectors:**

Consumer Discretionary, Energy, Healthcare, Industrials, Materials, Real Estate.

## 2. Likely Plan of Action for the Day Two, Week Two, or Month Two After This Pattern Occurs:

There's a 50-50 chance that one of these two outcomes will happen:

"You will have three opportunities to profit with this stock or index."

**OR**

"Defense and Real Estate stocks have a higher probability of success."

# Action 9

| Date | Price | Action | Sign/ Candle |
|---|---|---|---|
| End Date D6 | P6 | P6>P5 | +/Green/White Candle |
| D5 | P5 | P5>P4 | +/Green/White Candle |
| D4 | P4 | P4<P3 | - /Red/Black Candle |
| D3 | P3 | P3>P2 | +/Green/White Candle |
| D2 | P2 | P2>P1 | +/Green/White Candle |
| D1 | P1 | P1>P0 | +/Green/White Candle |
| Start Date D0 | P0 | | |

**The I Ching Says:**

**1a. Possible Plan of Action for the Day, Week, or Month After This Pattern Occurs:**

"Trading in this stock or index may result in an initial loss, but subsequent trades can be profitable."

**1b. Check out these Sectors:**

Consumer Discretionary, Consumer Staples, Financial Services, Industrials, Materials, Technology, Telecommunication Services.

**2. Likely Plan of Action for the Day Two, Week Two, or Month Two After This Pattern Occurs:**

There's a 50-50 chance that one of these two outcomes will happen:

"Consider stocks with high momentum and volatility. Having a well-defined plan with proper entry/exit targets and trailing stop loss can lead to profitability."

**OR**

"Expect probable success."

## Action 10

| Date | Price | Action | Sign/ Candle |
|---|---|---|---|
| End Date D6 | P6 | P6>P5 | +/Green/White Candle |
| D5 | P5 | P5>P4 | +/Green/White Candle |
| D4 | P4 | P4>P3 | +/Green/White Candle |
| D3 | P3 | P3<P2 | - /Red/Black Candle |
| D2 | P2 | P2>P1 | +/Green/White Candle |
| D1 | P1 | P1>P0 | +/Green/White Candle |
| Start Date D0 | P0 | | |

**The I Ching Says:**

**1a. Possible Plan of Action for the Day, Week, or Month After This Pattern Occurs:**

"Consider stocks with high momentum and volatility. Having a well-defined plan with proper entry/exit targets and trailing stop loss can lead to profitability."

**1b. Check out these Sectors:**

Consumer Discretionary, Consumer Staples, Financial Services, Healthcare, Industrials, Materials.

**2. Likely Plan of Action for the Day Two, Week Two, or Month Two After This Pattern Occurs:**

There's a 50-50 chance that one of these two outcomes will happen:

"If a previously 'weak' stock suddenly gains attention, trading it can lead to success. For other stock categories or indices, check whether they are above or below the 200-period moving average, near or crossing 52-week highs, or nearing 52-week lows, or if their support/resistance levels have been breached."

**OR**

"Anticipate small profits, but only at the end of the timeframe period."

# Action 11

| Date | Price | Action | Sign/ Candle |
|---|---|---|---|
| End Date D6 | P6 | P6<P5 | - /Red/Black Candle |
| D5 | P5 | P5<P4 | - /Red/Black Candle |
| D4 | P4 | P4<P3 | - /Red/Black Candle |
| D3 | P3 | P3>P2 | +/Green/White Candle |
| D2 | P2 | P2>P1 | +/Green/White Candle |
| D1 | P1 | P1>P0 | +/Green/White Candle |
| Start Date D0 | P0 | | |

**The I Ching Says:**

**1a. Possible Plan of Action for the Day, Week, or Month After This Pattern Occurs:**

"Taking a long position in this stock/index is likely to be more profitable than selling short."

**1b. Check out these Sectors:**

Consumer Discretionary, Financial Services, Healthcare, Industrials, Materials, Real Estate.

**2. Likely Plan of Action for the Day Two, Week Two, or Month Two After This Pattern Occurs:**

There's a 50-50 chance that one of these two outcomes will happen:

"Anticipate initial losses, but potential profits later."

**OR**

"This pattern is more applicable for daily candlesticks and daily time periods. Avoid holding the position for more than eight days."

# Action 12

| Date | Price | Action | Sign/ Candle |
|---|---|---|---|
| End Date D6 | P6 | P6>P5 | +/Green/White Candle |
| D5 | P5 | P5>P4 | +/Green/White Candle |
| D4 | P4 | P4>P3 | +/Green/White Candle |
| D3 | P3 | P3<P2 | - /Red/Black Candle |
| D2 | P2 | P2<P1 | - /Red/Black Candle |
| D1 | P1 | P1<P0 | - /Red/Black Candle |
| Start Date D0 | P0 | | |

**The I Ching Says:**

**1a. Possible Plan of Action for the Day, Week, or Month After This Pattern Occurs:**

"The stock is currently in a consolidation phase, experiencing stagnation."

**1b. Check out these Sectors:**

Consumer Discretionary, Financial Services, Healthcare, Industrials, Materials, Real Estate.

## 2. Likely Plan of Action for the Day Two, Week Two, or Month Two After This Pattern Occurs:

There's a 50-50 chance that one of these two outcomes will happen:

"If your stock is a small-cap stock, your trade is likely to be profitable."

**OR**

"If your stock is from the Consumer Discretionary sector and is currently trending, there's a probable chance of success."

| Date | Price | Action | Sign/ Candle |
|---|---|---|---|
| End Date D6 | P6 | P6>P5 | +/Green/White Candle |
| D5 | P5 | P5>P4 | +/Green/White Candle |
| D4 | P4 | P4>P3 | +/Green/White Candle |
| D3 | P3 | P3>P2 | +/Green/White Candle |
| D2 | P2 | P2<P1 | - /Red/Black Candle |
| D1 | P1 | P1>P0 | +/Green/White Candle |
| Start Date D0 | P0 | | |

**The I Ching Says:**

**1a. Possible Plan of Action for the Day, Week, or Month After This Pattern Occurs:**

"If a previously 'weak' stock suddenly gains attention, trading it can lead to success. For other stock categories or indices, check whether they are above or below the 200-period moving average, near or crossing 52-week highs, or nearing 52-week lows, or if their support/resistance levels have been breached."

**1b. Check out these Sectors:**

Consumer Discretionary, Consumer Staples, Financial Services, Healthcare, Industrials, Materials, Technology, Telecommunication Services, Utilities.

**2. Likely Plan of Action for the Day Two, Week Two, or Month Two After This Pattern Occurs:**

There's a 50-50 chance that one of these two outcomes will happen:

"Exercise patience and wait."

**OR**

"Check whether the stock is in an overbought or oversold condition before making a decision."

# Action 14

| Date | Price | Action | Sign/ Candle |
|---|---|---|---|
| End Date D6 | P6 | P6>P5 | +/Green/White Candle |
| D5 | P5 | P5<P4 | - /Red/Black Candle |
| D4 | P4 | P4>P3 | +/Green/White Candle |
| D3 | P3 | P3>P2 | +/Green/White Candle |
| D2 | P2 | P2>P1 | +/Green/White Candle |
| D1 | P1 | P1>P0 | +/Green/White Candle |
| Start Date D0 | P0 | | |

**The I Ching Says:**

**1a. Possible Plan of Action for the Day, Week, or Month After This Pattern Occurs:**

"Expect a high likelihood of success."

**1b. Check out these Sectors:**

Consumer Discretionary, Consumer Staples, Financial Services, Healthcare, Industrials, Materials, Technology, Telecommunication Services, Utilities.

## 2. Likely Plan of Action for the Day Two, Week Two, or Month Two After This Pattern Occurs:

There's a 50-50 chance that one of these two outcomes will happen:

"Trading in this stock or index may result in an initial loss, but subsequent trades can be profitable."

### OR

"Avoid taking immediate action. Observe the stock's trend. Wait for the candle to close above the resistance level or below the support level before taking any action."

# Action 15

| Date | Price | Action | Sign/ Candle |
| --- | --- | --- | --- |
| End Date D6 | P6 | P6<P5 | - /Red/Black Candle |
| D5 | P5 | P5<P4 | - /Red/Black Candle |
| D4 | P4 | P4<P3 | - /Red/Black Candle |
| D3 | P3 | P3>P2 | +/Green/White Candle |
| D2 | P2 | P2<P1 | - /Red/Black Candle |
| D1 | P1 | P1<P0 | - /Red/Black Candle |
| Start Date D0 | P0 | | |

**The I Ching Says:**

**1a. Possible Plan of Action for the Day, Week, or Month After This Pattern Occurs:**

"Opting for a trending stock will enhance the chances of success."

**1b. Check out these Sectors:**

Consumer Discretionary, Consumer Staples, Healthcare, Industrials, Materials, Real Estate.

## 2. Likely Plan of Action for the Day Two, Week Two, or Month Two After This Pattern Occurs:

There's a 50-50 chance that one of these two outcomes will happen:

"Stocks may experience a gap up or down, leading to price volatility. Carefully monitor the situation for an opportunity before making a move. This can lead to profitable outcomes."

**OR**

"Selecting a leading stock in an active sector can yield profits, but patience is required."

# Action 16

| Date | Price | Action | Sign/ Candle |
| --- | --- | --- | --- |
| End Date D6 | P6 | P6<P5 | - /Red/Black Candle |
| D5 | P5 | P5<P4 | - /Red/Black Candle |
| D4 | P4 | P4>P3 | +/Green/White Candle |
| D3 | P3 | P3<P2 | - /Red/Black Candle |
| D2 | P2 | P2<P1 | - /Red/Black Candle |
| D1 | P1 | P1<P0 | - /Red/Black Candle |
| Start Date D0 | P0 | | |

**The I Ching Says:**

**1a. Possible Plan of Action for the Day, Week, or Month After This Pattern Occurs:**

"Defense and Real Estate stocks have a higher probability of success."

**1b. Check out these Sectors:**

Consumer Discretionary, Energy, Healthcare, Industrials, Materials, Real Estate, Technology, Telecommunication Services, Utilities.

## 2. Likely Plan of Action for the Day Two, Week Two, or Month Two After This Pattern Occurs:

There's a 50-50 chance that one of these two outcomes will happen:

"Exercise patience and wait."

**OR**

"Opting for a trending stock will enhance the chances of success."

# Action 17

| Date | Price | Action | Sign/ Candle |
|---|---|---|---|
| End Date D6 | P6 | P6<P5 | - /Red/Black Candle |
| D5 | P5 | P5>P4 | +/Green/White Candle |
| D4 | P4 | P4>P3 | +/Green/White Candle |
| D3 | P3 | P3<P2 | - /Red/Black Candle |
| D2 | P2 | P2<P1 | - /Red/Black Candle |
| D1 | P1 | P1>P0 | +/Green/White Candle |
| Start Date D0 | P0 | | |

**The I Ching Says:**

**1a. Possible Plan of Action for the Day, Week, or Month After This Pattern Occurs:**

"Follow the prevailing trend to make a profit."

**1b. Check out these Sectors:**

Consumer Discretionary, Energy, Financial Services, Healthcare, Industrials, Materials, Real Estate, Technology, Telecommunication Services, Utilities.

## 2. Likely Plan of Action for the Day Two, Week Two, or Month Two After This Pattern Occurs:

There's a 50-50 chance that one of these two outcomes will happen:

"Stocks with momentum may yield small profits."

**OR**

"If your stock is a small-cap stock from a trending sector, your trade is likely to be profitable. Avoid large caps."

**Action 18**

| Date | Price | Action | Sign/ Candle |
|---|---|---|---|
| End Date D6 | P6 | P6>P5 | +/Green/White Candle |
| D5 | P5 | P5<P4 | - /Red/Black Candle |
| D4 | P4 | P4<P3 | - /Red/Black Candle |
| D3 | P3 | P3>P2 | +/Green/White Candle |
| D2 | P2 | P2>P1 | +/Green/White Candle |
| D1 | P1 | P1<P0 | - /Red/Black Candle |
| Start Date D0 | P0 | | |

**The I Ching Says:**

**1a. Possible Plan of Action for the Day, Week, or Month After This Pattern Occurs:**

"If a stock was previously in a consolidation phase and is now breaking through its resistance or support levels, there's a high probability of success."

**1b. Check out these Sectors:**

Consumer Discretionary, Consumer Staples, Industrials, Materials, Real Estate, Technology, Telecommunication Services.

**2. Likely Plan of Action for the Day Two, Week Two, or Month Two After This Pattern Occurs:**

There's a 50-50 chance that one of these two outcomes will happen:

"If your stock is above or below the 200-period moving average, near or crossing 52-week highs, or nearing 52-week lows, or if its support/resistance levels have been breached, then consider it."

**OR**

"Exercise patience and wait."

# Action 19

| Date | Price | Action | Sign/ Candle |
|---|---|---|---|
| End Date D6 | P6 | P6<P5 | - /Red/Black Candle |
| D5 | P5 | P5<P4 | - /Red/Black Candle |
| D4 | P4 | P4<P3 | - /Red/Black Candle |
| D3 | P3 | P3<P2 | - /Red/Black Candle |
| D2 | P2 | P2>P1 | +/Green/White Candle |
| D1 | P1 | P1>P0 | +/Green/White Candle |
| Start Date D0 | P0 | | |

**The I Ching Says:**

**1a. Possible Plan of Action for the Day, Week, or Month After This Pattern Occurs:**

"This pattern is more applicable for daily candlesticks and daily time periods. Avoid holding the position for more than eight days."

**1b. Check out these Sectors:**

Consumer Discretionary, Financial Services, Healthcare, Industrials, Materials, Real Estate, Telecommunication Services.

**2. Likely Plan of Action for the Day Two, Week Two, or Month Two After This Pattern Occurs:**

There's a 50-50 chance that one of these two outcomes will happen:

"If your stock is a market leader, there's a probable chance of success."

**OR**

"Buy with a small exit target in mind."

**Action 20**

| Date | Price | Action | Sign/ Candle |
|---|---|---|---|
| End Date D6 | P6 | P6>P5 | +/Green/White Candle |
| D5 | P5 | P5>P4 | +/Green/White Candle |
| D4 | P4 | P4<P3 | - /Red/Black Candle |
| D3 | P3 | P3<P2 | - /Red/Black Candle |
| D2 | P2 | P2<P1 | - /Red/Black Candle |
| D1 | P1 | P1<P0 | - /Red/Black Candle |
| Start Date D0 | P0 | | |

**The I Ching Says:**

**1a. Possible Plan of Action for the Day, Week, or Month After This Pattern Occurs:**

"Exercise patience and wait."

**1b. Check out these Sectors:**

Consumer Discretionary, Consumer Staples, Financial Services, Healthcare, Industrials, Materials, Real Estate, Technology, Telecommunication Services, Utilities.

## 2. Likely Plan of Action for the Day Two, Week Two, or Month Two After This Pattern Occurs:

There's a 50-50 chance that one of these two outcomes will happen:

"The stock is currently in a consolidation phase, experiencing stagnation."

### OR

"Select a trending stock for a higher chance of success."

# Action 21

| Date | Price | Action | Sign/ Candle |
|---|---|---|---|
| End Date D6 | P6 | P6>P5 | +/Green/White Candle |
| D5 | P5 | P5<P4 | - /Red/Black Candle |
| D4 | P4 | P4>P3 | +/Green/White Candle |
| D3 | P3 | P3<P2 | - /Red/Black Candle |
| D2 | P2 | P2<P1 | - /Red/Black Candle |
| D1 | P1 | P1>P0 | +/Green/White Candle |
| Start Date D0 | P0 | | |

**The I Ching Says:**

**1a. Possible Plan of Action for the Day, Week, or Month After This Pattern Occurs:**

"Maintain patience and wait."

**1b. Check out these Sectors:**

Consumer Discretionary, Consumer Staples, Financial Services, Healthcare, Industrials, Materials, Real Estate, Technology, Telecommunication Services, Utilities.

## 2. Likely Plan of Action for the Day Two, Week Two, or Month Two After This Pattern Occurs:

There's a 50-50 chance that one of these two outcomes will happen:

"If your stock is from the Consumer Discretionary sector and is currently trending, there's a probable chance of success."

### OR

"Expect a probable loss if you trade in this stock. Seek advice from a market professional."

| Date | Price | Action | Sign/ Candle |
|---|---|---|---|
| End Date D6 | P6 | P6>P5 | +/Green/White Candle |
| D5 | P5 | P5<P4 | - /Red/Black Candle |
| D4 | P4 | P4<P3 | - /Red/Black Candle |
| D3 | P3 | P3>P2 | +/Green/White Candle |
| D2 | P2 | P2<P1 | - /Red/Black Candle |
| D1 | P1 | P1>P0 | +/Green/White Candle |
| Start Date D0 | P0 | | |

**The I Ching Says:**

**1a. Possible Plan of Action for the Day, Week, or Month After This Pattern Occurs:**

"Small profits are possible with proper money management."

**1b. Check out these Sectors:**

Consumer Discretionary, Consumer Staples, Financial Services, Healthcare, Industrials,

Materials, Real Estate, Technology, Telecommunication Services, Utilities.

## 2. Likely Plan of Action for the Day Two, Week Two, or Month Two After This Pattern Occurs:

There's a 50-50 chance that one of these two outcomes will happen:

"If your stock is above or below the 200-period moving average, near or crossing 52-week highs, or nearing 52-week lows, or if its support/resistance levels have been breached, then consider it."

**OR**

"Expect a probable loss ahead."

**Action 23**

| Date | Price | Action | Sign/ Candle |
| --- | --- | --- | --- |
| End Date D6 | P6 | P6>P5 | +/Green/White Candle |
| D5 | P5 | P5<P4 | - /Red/Black Candle |
| D4 | P4 | P4<P3 | - /Red/Black Candle |
| D3 | P3 | P3<P2 | - /Red/Black Candle |
| D2 | P2 | P2<P1 | - /Red/Black Candle |
| D1 | P1 | P1<P0 | - /Red/Black Candle |
| Start Date D0 | P0 | | |

**The I Ching Says:**

**1a. Possible Plan of Action for the Day, Week, or Month After This Pattern Occurs:**

"Exercise caution and anticipate a correction period ahead."

**1b. Check out these Sectors:**

Consumer Discretionary, Consumer Staples, Healthcare, Industrials, Materials, Real Estate.

## 2. Likely Plan of Action for the Day Two, Week Two, or Month Two After This Pattern Occurs:

There's a 50-50 chance that one of these two outcomes will happen:

"Exercise patience and wait."

**OR**

"Trade stocks that are trending, have gaps up or down, and avoid laggards."

| Date | Price | Action | Sign/ Candle |
|---|---|---|---|
| End Date D6 | P6 | P6<P5 | - /Red/Black Candle |
| D5 | P5 | P5<P4 | - /Red/Black Candle |
| D4 | P4 | P4<P3 | - /Red/Black Candle |
| D3 | P3 | P3<P2 | - /Red/Black Candle |
| D2 | P2 | P2<P1 | - /Red/Black Candle |
| D1 | P1 | P1>P0 | +/Green/White Candle |
| Start Date D0 | P0 | | |

**The I Ching Says:**

**1a. Possible Plan of Action for the Day, Week, or Month After This Pattern Occurs:**

"Buy with a small exit target in mind."

**1b. Check out these Sectors:**

Consumer Discretionary, Energy, Healthcare, Industrials, Materials, Real Estate, Technology, Telecommunication Services, Utilities.

## 2. Likely Plan of Action for the Day Two, Week Two, or Month Two After This Pattern Occurs:

There's a 50-50 chance that one of these two outcomes will happen:

"Exercise caution and anticipate a correction period ahead."

### OR

"What goes down will come up. This is known as the 'reversion to the mean' theory. This pattern works best with daily candlesticks. Once the lowest candle is formed, place a buy order above the high of this candle. Set an exit target and a trailing stop loss."

# Action 25

| Date | Price | Action | Sign/ Candle |
|---|---|---|---|
| End Date D6 | P6 | P6>P5 | +/Green/White Candle |
| D5 | P5 | P5>P4 | +/Green/White Candle |
| D4 | P4 | P4>P3 | +/Green/White Candle |
| D3 | P3 | P3<P2 | - /Red/Black Candle |
| D2 | P2 | P2<P1 | - /Red/Black Candle |
| D1 | P1 | P1>P0 | +/Green/White Candle |
| Start Date D0 | P0 | | |

**The I Ching Says:**

**1a. Possible Plan of Action for the Day, Week, or Month After This Pattern Occurs:**

"Select a trending stock for a better chance of success."

**1b. Check out these Sectors:**

Consumer Discretionary, Energy, Financial Services, Industrials, Real Estate, Technology, Telecommunication Services, Utilities.

**2. Likely Plan of Action for the Day Two, Week Two, or Month Two After This Pattern Occurs:**

There's a 50-50 chance that one of these two outcomes will happen:

"If your stock is a small-cap stock, your trade is likely to be profitable."

**OR**

"If your stock is from the Consumer Discretionary sector and is currently trending, there's a probable chance of success."

| Date | Price | Action | Sign/ Candle |
|---|---|---|---|
| End Date D6 | P6 | P6>P5 | +/Green/White Candle |
| D5 | P5 | P5<P4 | - /Red/Black Candle |
| D4 | P4 | P4<P3 | - /Red/Black Candle |
| D3 | P3 | P3>P2 | +/Green/White Candle |
| D2 | P2 | P2>P1 | +/Green/White Candle |
| D1 | P1 | P1>P0 | +/Green/White Candle |
| Start Date D0 | P0 | | |

**The I Ching Says:**

**1a. Possible Plan of Action for the Day, Week, or Month After This Pattern Occurs:**

"If your stock is a trending foreign stock, there's a probable chance of success."

**1b. Check out these Sectors:**

Consumer Discretionary, Consumer Staples, Industrials, Real Estate, Utilities.

**2. Likely Plan of Action for the Day Two, Week Two, or Month Two After This Pattern Occurs:**

There's a 50-50 chance that one of these two outcomes will happen:

"If your stock is above or below the 200-period moving average, near or crossing 52-week highs, or nearing 52-week lows, or if its support / resistance levels have been breached, then consider it."

**OR**

"Exercise patience and wait."

# Action 27

| Date | Price | Action | Sign/ Candle |
|---|---|---|---|
| End Date D6 | P6 | P6>P5 | +/Green/White Candle |
| D5 | P5 | P5<P4 | - /Red/Black Candle |
| D4 | P4 | P4<P3 | - /Red/Black Candle |
| D3 | P3 | P3<P2 | - /Red/Black Candle |
| D2 | P2 | P2<P1 | - /Red/Black Candle |
| D1 | P1 | P1>P0 | +/Green/White Candle |
| Start Date D0 | P0 | | |

**The I Ching Says:**

**1a. Possible Plan of Action for the Day, Week, or Month After This Pattern Occurs:**

"If your stock is a market leader, there's a probable chance of success."

**1b. Check out these Sectors:**

Consumer Discretionary, Consumer Staples, Energy, Industrials, Real Estate, Technology, Telecommunication Services, Utilities.

## 2. Likely Plan of Action for the Day Two, Week Two, or Month Two After This Pattern Occurs:

There's a 50-50 chance that one of these two outcomes will happen:

"Exercise patience and wait."

**OR**

"Trade stocks that are trending, have gaps up or down, and avoid laggards."

| Date | Price | Action | Sign/ Candle |
|---|---|---|---|
| End Date D6 | P6 | P6<P5 | - /Red/Black Candle |
| D5 | P5 | P5>P4 | +/Green/White Candle |
| D4 | P4 | P4>P3 | +/Green/White Candle |
| D3 | P3 | P3>P2 | +/Green/White Candle |
| D2 | P2 | P2>P1 | +/Green/White Candle |
| D1 | P1 | P1<P0 | - /Red/Black Candle |
| Start Date D0 | P0 | | |

**The I Ching Says:**

**1a. Possible Plan of Action for the Day, Week, or Month After This Pattern Occurs:**

"Check whether the stock is in an overbought or oversold condition before making a decision."

**1b. Check out these Sectors:**

Consumer Discretionary, Consumer Staples, Financial Services, Healthcare, Industrials,

Materials, Technology, Telecommunication Services.

## 2. Likely Plan of Action for the Day Two, Week Two, or Month Two After This Pattern Occurs:

There's a 50-50 chance that one of these two outcomes will happen:

"Expect a high likelihood of success."

## OR

"If your stock is a large-cap stock, your trade is likely to be profitable."

# Action 29

| Date | Price | Action | Sign/ Candle |
|---|---|---|---|
| End Date D6 | P6 | P6<P5 | - /Red/Black Candle |
| D5 | P5 | P5>P4 | +/Green/White Candle |
| D4 | P4 | P4<P3 | - /Red/Black Candle |
| D3 | P3 | P3<P2 | - /Red/Black Candle |
| D2 | P2 | P2>P1 | +/Green/White Candle |
| D1 | P1 | P1<P0 | - /Red/Black Candle |
| Start Date D0 | P0 | | |

**The I Ching Says:**

**1a. Possible Plan of Action for the Day, Week, or Month After This Pattern Occurs:**

"Expect a probable loss ahead."

**1b. Check out these Sectors:**

Consumer Discretionary, Energy, Healthcare, Industrials, Materials.

## 2. Likely Plan of Action for the Day Two, Week Two, or Month Two After This Pattern Occurs:

There's a 50-50 chance that one of these two outcomes will happen:

"Maintain patience and wait."

**OR**

"Price swings may occur."

# Action 30

| Date | Price | Action | Sign/ Candle |
|---|---|---|---|
| End Date D6 | P6 | P6>P5 | +/Green/White Candle |
| D5 | P5 | P5<P4 | - /Red/Black Candle |
| D4 | P4 | P4>P3 | +/Green/White Candle |
| D3 | P3 | P3>P2 | +/Green/White Candle |
| D2 | P2 | P2<P1 | - /Red/Black Candle |
| D1 | P1 | P1<P0 | - /Red/Black Candle |
| Start Date D0 | P0 | | |

**The I Ching Says:**

**1a. Possible Plan of Action for the Day, Week, or Month After This Pattern Occurs:**

"If your stock is from a dividend-paying company in either the Consumer Discretionary or Consumer Staples sectors, whichever is trending, there's a probable chance of success."

**1b. Check out these Sectors:**

Consumer Discretionary, Consumer Staples, Financial Services, Healthcare, Industrials, Materials, Technology, Telecommunication Services, Utilities.

## 2. Likely Plan of Action for the Day Two, Week Two, or Month Two After This Pattern Occurs:

There's a 50-50 chance that one of these two outcomes will happen:

"You can achieve a small profit with proper money management in place."

**OR**

"Prepare for a loss."

# Action 31

| Date | Price | Action | Sign/ Candle |
|---|---|---|---|
| End Date D6 | P6 | P6<P5 | - /Red/Black Candle |
| D5 | P5 | P5>P4 | +/Green/White Candle |
| D4 | P4 | P4>P3 | +/Green/White Candle |
| D3 | P3 | P3>P2 | +/Green/White Candle |
| D2 | P2 | P2<P1 | - /Red/Black Candle |
| D1 | P1 | P1<P0 | - /Red/Black Candle |
| Start Date D0 | P0 | | |

**The I Ching Says:**

**1a. Possible Plan of Action for the Day, Week, or Month After This Pattern Occurs:**

"If your stock is from the Consumer Discretionary sector and is currently trending, there's a probable chance of success."

**1b. Check out these Sectors:**

Consumer Discretionary, Consumer Staples, Financial Services, Healthcare, Industrials,

Materials, Technology, Telecommunication Services, Utilities.

## 2. Likely Plan of Action for the Day Two, Week Two, or Month Two After This Pattern Occurs:

There's a 50-50 chance that one of these two outcomes will happen:

"Expect probable success."

### OR

"Proper money management is crucial for this stock."

# Action 32

| Date | Price | Action | Sign/ Candle |
| --- | --- | --- | --- |
| End Date D6 | P6 | P6<P5 | - /Red/Black Candle |
| D5 | P5 | P5<P4 | - /Red/Black Candle |
| D4 | P4 | P4>P3 | +/Green/White Candle |
| D3 | P3 | P3>P2 | +/Green/White Candle |
| D2 | P2 | P2>P1 | +/Green/White Candle |
| D1 | P1 | P1<P0 | - /Red/Black Candle |
| Start Date D0 | P0 | | |

**The I Ching Says:**

**1a. Possible Plan of Action for the Day, Week, or Month After This Pattern Occurs:**

"Proper money management is crucial for this stock."

**1b. Check out these Sectors:**

Consumer Discretionary, Consumer Staples, Energy, Industrials, Materials, Real Estate,

Technology, Telecommunication Services, Utilities.

## 2. Likely Plan of Action for the Day Two, Week Two, or Month Two After This Pattern Occurs:

There's a 50-50 chance that one of these two outcomes will happen:

"If your stock is a trending foreign stock, there's a probable chance of success."

**OR**

"Taking a long position in this stock/index is likely to be more profitable than selling short."

# Action 33

| Date | Price | Action | Sign/ Candle |
|---|---|---|---|
| End Date D6 | P6 | P6>P5 | +/Green/White Candle |
| D5 | P5 | P5>P4 | +/Green/White Candle |
| D4 | P4 | P4>P3 | +/Green/White Candle |
| D3 | P3 | P3>P2 | +/Green/White Candle |
| D2 | P2 | P2<P1 | - /Red/Black Candle |
| D1 | P1 | P1<P0 | - /Red/Black Candle |
| Start Date D0 | P0 | | |

**The I Ching Says:**

**1a. Possible Plan of Action for the Day, Week, or Month After This Pattern Occurs:**

"If your stock is a small-cap stock, your trade is likely to be profitable."

**1b. Check out these Sectors:**

Consumer Discretionary, Consumer Staples, Financial Services, Industrials, Real Estate.

## 2. Likely Plan of Action for the Day Two, Week Two, or Month Two After This Pattern Occurs:

There's a 50-50 chance that one of these two outcomes will happen:

"Exercise patience and wait."

**OR**

"Check whether the stock is in an overbought or oversold condition before making a decision."

# Action 34

| Date | Price | Action | Sign/ Candle |
|---|---|---|---|
| End Date D6 | P6 | P6<P5 | - /Red/Black Candle |
| D5 | P5 | P5<P4 | - /Red/Black Candle |
| D4 | P4 | P4>P3 | +/Green/White Candle |
| D3 | P3 | P3>P2 | +/Green/White Candle |
| D2 | P2 | P2>P1 | +/Green/White Candle |
| D1 | P1 | P1>P0 | +/Green/White Candle |
| Start Date D0 | P0 | | |

**The I Ching Says:**

**1a. Possible Plan of Action for the Day, Week, or Month After This Pattern Occurs:**

"If your stock is a large-cap stock, your trade is likely to be profitable."

**1b. Check out these Sectors:**

Consumer Discretionary, Energy, Financial Services, Industrials, Real Estate, Technology, Telecommunication Services, Utilities.

**2. Likely Plan of Action for the Day Two, Week Two, or Month Two After This Pattern Occurs:**

There's a 50-50 chance that one of these two outcomes will happen:

"If your stock is a trending foreign stock, there's a probable chance of success."

**OR**

"Taking a long position in this stock/index is likely to be more profitable than selling short."

# Action 35

| Date | Price | Action | Sign/ Candle |
|---|---|---|---|
| End Date D6 | P6 | P6>P5 | +/Green/White Candle |
| D5 | P5 | P5<P4 | - /Red/Black Candle |
| D4 | P4 | P4>P3 | +/Green/White Candle |
| D3 | P3 | P3<P2 | - /Red/Black Candle |
| D2 | P2 | P2<P1 | - /Red/Black Candle |
| D1 | P1 | P1<P0 | - /Red/Black Candle |
| Start Date D0 | P0 | | |

**The I Ching Says:**

**1a. Possible Plan of Action for the Day, Week, or Month After This Pattern Occurs:**

"You will have three opportunities to profit with this stock or index."

**1b. Check out these Sectors:**

Consumer Discretionary, Consumer Staples, Financial Services, Healthcare, Industrials,

Materials, Real Estate, Technology, Telecommunication Services, Utilities.

## 2. Likely Plan of Action for the Day Two, Week Two, or Month Two After This Pattern Occurs:

There's a 50-50 chance that one of these two outcomes will happen:

"If your stock is from the Consumer Discretionary sector and is currently trending, there's a probable chance of success."

**OR**

"Expect a probable loss if you trade in this stock. Seek advice from a market professional."

# Action 36

| Date | Price | Action | Sign/ Candle |
|---|---|---|---|
| End Date D6 | P6 | P6<P5 | - /Red/Black Candle |
| D5 | P5 | P5<P4 | - /Red/Black Candle |
| D4 | P4 | P4<P3 | - /Red/Black Candle |
| D3 | P3 | P3>P2 | +/Green/White Candle |
| D2 | P2 | P2<P1 | - /Red/Black Candle |
| D1 | P1 | P1>P0 | +/Green/White Candle |
| Start Date D0 | P0 | | |

**The I Ching Says:**

**1a. Possible Plan of Action for the Day, Week, or Month After This Pattern Occurs:**

"Expect probable stagnation or a downslide for this stock."

**1b. Check out these Sectors:**

Consumer Discretionary, Consumer Staples, Financial Services, Healthcare, Industrials,

Materials, Real Estate, Technology, Telecommunication Services, Utilities.

## 2. Likely Plan of Action for the Day Two, Week Two, or Month Two After This Pattern Occurs:

There's a 50-50 chance that one of these two outcomes will happen:

"Stocks may experience a gap up or down, leading to price volatility. Carefully monitor the situation for an opportunity before making a move. This can lead to profitable outcomes."

**OR**

"Selecting a leading stock in an active sector can yield profits, but patience is required."

# Action 37

| Date | Price | Action | Sign/ Candle |
|---|---|---|---|
| End Date D6 | P6 | P6>P5 | +/Green/White Candle |
| D5 | P5 | P5>P4 | +/Green/White Candle |
| D4 | P4 | P4<P3 | - /Red/Black Candle |
| D3 | P3 | P3>P2 | +/Green/White Candle |
| D2 | P2 | P2<P1 | - /Red/Black Candle |
| D1 | P1 | P1>P0 | +/Green/White Candle |
| Start Date D0 | P0 | | |

**The I Ching Says:**

**1a. Possible Plan of Action for the Day, Week, or Month After This Pattern Occurs:**

"If your stock is from the Consumer Discretionary sector and is currently trending, there's a probable chance of success."

**1b. Check out these Sectors:**

Consumer Discretionary, Consumer Staples, Financial Services, Healthcare, Industrials,

Materials, Technology, Telecommunication Services, Utilities.

## 2. Likely Plan of Action for the Day Two, Week Two, or Month Two After This Pattern Occurs:

There's a 50-50 chance that one of these two outcomes will happen:

"Entering the market incorrectly carries a high probability of loss. Seek advice from a market professional."

**OR**

"Expect initial losses but potential profits later."

# Action 38

| Date | Price | Action | Sign/ Candle |
|---|---|---|---|
| End Date D6 | P6 | P6>P5 | +/Green/White Candle |
| D5 | P5 | P5<P4 | - /Red/Black Candle |
| D4 | P4 | P4>P3 | +/Green/White Candle |
| D3 | P3 | P3<P2 | - /Red/Black Candle |
| D2 | P2 | P2>P1 | +/Green/White Candle |
| D1 | P1 | P1>P0 | +/Green/White Candle |
| Start Date D0 | P0 | | |

**The I Ching Says:**

**1a. Possible Plan of Action for the Day, Week, or Month After This Pattern Occurs:**

"This stock is suitable for scalping."

**1b. Check out these Sectors:**

Consumer Discretionary, Consumer Staples, Financial Services, Healthcare, Industrials, Materials, Technology, Telecommunication Services, Utilities.

**2. Likely Plan of Action for the Day Two, Week Two, or Month Two After This Pattern Occurs:**

There's a 50-50 chance that one of these two outcomes will happen:

"If your stock is from the Consumer Discretionary sector and is currently trending, there's a probable chance of success."

**OR**

"Profits can turn into losses if you are not careful."

# Action 39

| Date | Price | Action | Sign/ Candle |
|---|---|---|---|
| End Date D6 | P6 | P6<P5 | - /Red/Black Candle |
| D5 | P5 | P5>P4 | +/Green/White Candle |
| D4 | P4 | P4<P3 | - /Red/Black Candle |
| D3 | P3 | P3>P2 | +/Green/White Candle |
| D2 | P2 | P2<P1 | - /Red/Black Candle |
| D1 | P1 | P1<P0 | - /Red/Black Candle |
| Start Date D0 | P0 | | |

**The I Ching Says:**

**1a. Possible Plan of Action for the Day, Week, or Month After This Pattern Occurs:**

"Expect a probable loss if you trade in this stock. Seek advice from a market professional."

**1b. Check out these Sectors:**

Consumer Discretionary, Consumer Staples, Energy, Healthcare, Industrials, Materials, Real Estate.

**2. Likely Plan of Action for the Day Two, Week Two, or Month Two After This Pattern Occurs:**

There's a 50-50 chance that one of these two outcomes will happen:

"Expect initial losses before making a profit if you trade in this stock."

**OR**

"Consider retreating if you have a position in this stock. If you possess great patience, then hold on."

# Action 40

| Date | Price | Action | Sign/ Candle |
|---|---|---|---|
| End Date D6 | P6 | P6<P5 | - /Red/Black Candle |
| D5 | P5 | P5<P4 | - /Red/Black Candle |
| D4 | P4 | P4>P3 | +/Green/White Candle |
| D3 | P3 | P3<P2 | - /Red/Black Candle |
| D2 | P2 | P2>P1 | +/Green/White Candle |
| D1 | P1 | P1<P0 | - /Red/Black Candle |
| Start Date D0 | P0 | | |

**The I Ching Says:**

**1a. Possible Plan of Action for the Day, Week, or Month After This Pattern Occurs:**

"Consider retreating if you have a position in this stock. If you possess great patience, then hold on."

**1b. Check out these Sectors:**

Consumer Discretionary, Energy, Healthcare, Industrials, Materials, Real Estate, Technology, Telecommunication Services, Utilities.

**2. Likely Plan of Action for the Day Two, Week Two, or Month Two After This Pattern Occurs:**

There's a 50-50 chance that one of these two outcomes will happen:

"Small profits are possible with proper money management."

**OR**

"Expect probable stagnation or a downslide for this stock."

# Action 41

| Date | Price | Action | Sign/ Candle |
|---|---|---|---|
| End Date D6 | P6 | P6>P5 | +/Green/White Candle |
| D5 | P5 | P5<P4 | - /Red/Black Candle |
| D4 | P4 | P4<P3 | - /Red/Black Candle |
| D3 | P3 | P3<P2 | - /Red/Black Candle |
| D2 | P2 | P2>P1 | +/Green/White Candle |
| D1 | P1 | P1>P0 | +/Green/White Candle |
| Start Date D0 | P0 | | |

**The I Ching Says:**

**1a. Possible Plan of Action for the Day, Week, or Month After This Pattern Occurs:**

"Anticipate initial losses, but potential profits later."

**1b. Check out these Sectors:**

Consumer Discretionary, Consumer Staples, Financial Services, Healthcare, Industrials,

Materials, Real Estate, Telecommunication Services.

## 2. Likely Plan of Action for the Day Two, Week Two, or Month Two After This Pattern Occurs:

There's a 50-50 chance that one of these two outcomes will happen:

"If your stock is above or below the 200-period moving average, near or crossing 52-week highs, or nearing 52-week lows, or if its support/resistance levels have been breached, then consider it."

### OR

"Maintain your current position. Expect initial resistance followed by success. Patience is necessary."

# Action 42

| Date | Price | Action | Sign/ Candle |
|---|---|---|---|
| End Date D6 | P6 | P6>P5 | +/Green/White Candle |
| D5 | P5 | P5>P4 | +/Green/White Candle |
| D4 | P4 | P4<P3 | - /Red/Black Candle |
| D3 | P3 | P3<P2 | - /Red/Black Candle |
| D2 | P2 | P2<P1 | - /Red/Black Candle |
| D1 | P1 | P1>P0 | +/Green/White Candle |
| Start Date D0 | P0 | | |

**The I Ching Says:**

**1a. Possible Plan of Action for the Day, Week, or Month After This Pattern Occurs:**

"If your stock is above or below the 200-period moving average, near or crossing 52-week highs, or nearing 52-week lows, or if its support/ resistance levels have been breached, then consider it."

**1b. Check out these Sectors:**

Consumer Discretionary, Consumer Staples, Energy, Industrials, Real Estate, Telecommunication Services.

**2. Likely Plan of Action for the Day Two, Week Two, or Month Two After This Pattern Occurs:**

There's a 50-50 chance that one of these two outcomes will happen:

"The stock is currently in a consolidation phase, experiencing stagnation."

**OR**

"Select a trending stock for a higher chance of success."

# Action 43

| Date | Price | Action | Sign/ Candle |
|---|---|---|---|
| End Date D6 | P6 | P6<P5 | - /Red/Black Candle |
| D5 | P5 | P5>P4 | +/Green/White Candle |
| D4 | P4 | P4>P3 | +/Green/White Candle |
| D3 | P3 | P3>P2 | +/Green/White Candle |
| D2 | P2 | P2>P1 | +/Green/White Candle |
| D1 | P1 | P1>P0 | +/Green/White Candle |
| Start Date D0 | P0 | | |

**The I Ching Says:**

**1a. Possible Plan of Action for the Day, Week, or Month After This Pattern Occurs:**

"Prepare for price swings and trade with proper money management."

**1b. Check out these Sectors:**

Consumer Discretionary, Financial Services, Healthcare, Industrials, Materials, Telecommunication Services.

## 2. Likely Plan of Action for the Day Two, Week Two, or Month Two After This Pattern Occurs:

There's a 50-50 chance that one of these two outcomes will happen:

"Expect a high likelihood of success."

### OR

"If your stock is a large-cap stock, your trade is likely to be profitable."

# Action 44

| Date | Price | Action | Sign/ Candle |
| --- | --- | --- | --- |
| End Date D6 | P6 | P6>P5 | +/Green/White Candle |
| D5 | P5 | P5>P4 | +/Green/White Candle |
| D4 | P4 | P4>P3 | +/Green/White Candle |
| D3 | P3 | P3>P2 | +/Green/White Candle |
| D2 | P2 | P2>P1 | +/Green/White Candle |
| D1 | P1 | P1<P0 | - /Red/Black Candle |
| Start Date D0 | P0 | | |

**The I Ching Says:**

**1a. Possible Plan of Action for the Day, Week, or Month After This Pattern Occurs:**

"Exercise patience and wait."

**1b. Check out these Sectors:**

Consumer Discretionary, Consumer Staples, Energy, Financial Services, Industrials, Materials, Technology.

## 2. Likely Plan of Action for the Day Two, Week Two, or Month Two After This Pattern Occurs:

There's a 50-50 chance that one of these two outcomes will happen:

"What goes up will come down. This is known as the 'reversion to the mean' theory. This pattern works best with daily candlesticks. Once the highest candle is formed, place a sell order below the low of this candle. Set an exit target and a trailing stop loss."

### OR

"Prepare for price swings and trade with proper money management."

# Action 45

| Date | Price | Action | Sign/ Candle |
|---|---|---|---|
| End Date D6 | P6 | P6<P5 | - /Red/Black Candle |
| D5 | P5 | P5>P4 | +/Green/White Candle |
| D4 | P4 | P4>P3 | +/Green/White Candle |
| D3 | P3 | P3<P2 | - /Red/Black Candle |
| D2 | P2 | P2<P1 | - /Red/Black Candle |
| D1 | P1 | P1<P0 | - /Red/Black Candle |
| Start Date D0 | P0 | | |

**The I Ching Says:**

**1a. Possible Plan of Action for the Day, Week, or Month After This Pattern Occurs:**

"Select a trending stock for a higher chance of success."

**1b. Check out these Sectors:**

Consumer Discretionary, Financial Services, Healthcare, Industrials, Materials, Real Estate, Technology, Telecommunication Services.

**2. Likely Plan of Action for the Day Two, Week Two, or Month Two After This Pattern Occurs:**

There's a 50-50 chance that one of these two outcomes will happen:

"Stocks with momentum may yield small profits."

**OR**

"If your stock is a small-cap stock from a trending sector, your trade is likely to be profitable. Avoid large caps."

# Action 46

| Date | Price | Action | Sign/ Candle |
|---|---|---|---|
| End Date D6 | P6 | P6<P5 | - /Red/Black Candle |
| D5 | P5 | P5<P4 | - /Red/Black Candle |
| D4 | P4 | P4<P3 | - /Red/Black Candle |
| D3 | P3 | P3>P2 | +/Green/White Candle |
| D2 | P2 | P2>P1 | +/Green/White Candle |
| D1 | P1 | P1<P0 | - /Red/Black Candle |
| Start Date D0 | P0 | | |

**The I Ching Says:**

**1a. Possible Plan of Action for the Day, Week, or Month After This Pattern Occurs:**

"This stock is likely to go up. Seek advice from a market professional."

**1b. Check out these Sectors:**

Consumer Discretionary, Consumer Staples, Healthcare, Industrials, Materials, Real Estate, Technology, Telecommunication Services.

## 2. Likely Plan of Action for the Day Two, Week Two, or Month Two After This Pattern Occurs:

There's a 50-50 chance that one of these two outcomes will happen:

"Anticipate initial losses, but potential profits later."

### OR

"This pattern is more applicable for daily candlesticks and daily time periods. Avoid holding the position for more than eight days."

# Action 47

| Date | Price | Action | Sign/ Candle |
|---|---|---|---|
| End Date D6 | P6 | P6<P5 | - /Red/Black Candle |
| D5 | P5 | P5>P4 | +/Green/White Candle |
| D4 | P4 | P4>P3 | +/Green/White Candle |
| D3 | P3 | P3<P2 | - /Red/Black Candle |
| D2 | P2 | P2>P1 | +/Green/White Candle |
| D1 | P1 | P1<P0 | - /Red/Black Candle |
| Start Date D0 | P0 | | |

**The I Ching Says:**

**1a. Possible Plan of Action for the Day, Week, or Month After This Pattern Occurs:**

"Expect initial losses but potential profits later."

**1b. Check out these Sectors:**

Consumer Discretionary, Energy, Financial Services, Healthcare, Industrials, Materials, Telecommunication Services.

## 2. Likely Plan of Action for the Day Two, Week Two, or Month Two After This Pattern Occurs:

There's a 50-50 chance that one of these two outcomes will happen:

"If your stock is from a dividend-paying company in either the Consumer Discretionary or Consumer Staples sectors, whichever is trending, there's a probable chance of success."

**OR**

"If your stock is a large-cap stock from a trending sector, your trade is likely to be profitable."

**Action 48**

| Date | Price | Action | Sign/ Candle |
|---|---|---|---|
| End Date D6 | P6 | P6<P5 | - /Red/Black Candle |
| D5 | P5 | P5>P4 | +/Green/White Candle |
| D4 | P4 | P4<P3 | - /Red/Black Candle |
| D3 | P3 | P3>P2 | +/Green/White Candle |
| D2 | P2 | P2>P1 | +/Green/White Candle |
| D1 | P1 | P1<P0 | - /Red/Black Candle |
| Start Date D0 | P0 | | |

**The I Ching Says:**

**1a. Possible Plan of Action for the Day, Week, or Month After This Pattern Occurs:**

"Prepare for a loss."

**1b. Check out these Sectors:**

Consumer Discretionary, Consumer Staples, Energy, Healthcare, Industrials, Materials, Technology, Telecommunication Services.

**2. Likely Plan of Action for the Day Two, Week Two, or Month Two After This Pattern Occurs:**

There's a 50-50 chance that one of these two outcomes will happen:

"This stock is suitable for scalping."

**OR**

"If your stock is from the Consumer Discretionary sector and is currently trending, there's a probable chance of loss."

# Action 49

| Date | Price | Action | Sign/ Candle |
| --- | --- | --- | --- |
| End Date D6 | P6 | P6<P5 | - /Red/Black Candle |
| D5 | P5 | P5>P4 | +/Green/White Candle |
| D4 | P4 | P4>P3 | +/Green/White Candle |
| D3 | P3 | P3>P2 | +/Green/White Candle |
| D2 | P2 | P2<P1 | - /Red/Black Candle |
| D1 | P1 | P1>P0 | +/Green/White Candle |
| Start Date D0 | P0 | | |

**The I Ching Says:**

**1a. Possible Plan of Action for the Day, Week, or Month After This Pattern Occurs:**

"Anticipate small profits, but only at the end of the timeframe period."

**1b. Check out these Sectors:**

Consumer Discretionary, Consumer Staples, Financial Services, Healthcare, Industrials,

Materials, Technology, Telecommunication Services, Utilities.

## 2. Likely Plan of Action for the Day Two, Week Two, or Month Two After This Pattern Occurs:

There's a 50-50 chance that one of these two outcomes will happen:

"Expect probable success."

### OR

"Proper money management is crucial for this stock."

# Action 50

| Date | Price | Action | Sign/ Candle |
| --- | --- | --- | --- |
| End Date D6 | P6 | P6>P5 | +/Green/White Candle |
| D5 | P5 | P5<P4 | - /Red/Black Candle |
| D4 | P4 | P4>P3 | +/Green/White Candle |
| D3 | P3 | P3>P2 | +/Green/White Candle |
| D2 | P2 | P2>P1 | +/Green/White Candle |
| D1 | P1 | P1<P0 | - /Red/Black Candle |
| Start Date D0 | P0 | | |

**The I Ching Says:**

**1a. Possible Plan of Action for the Day, Week, or Month After This Pattern Occurs:**

"Expect probable success."

**1b. Check out these Sectors:**

Consumer Discretionary, Consumer Staples, Financial Services, Healthcare, Industrials, Materials, Technology, Telecommunication Services, Utilities.

## 2. Likely Plan of Action for the Day Two, Week Two, or Month Two After This Pattern Occurs:

There's a 50-50 chance that one of these two outcomes will happen:

"Trading in this stock or index may result in an initial loss, but subsequent trades can be profitable."

**OR**

"Avoid taking immediate action. Observe the stock's trend. Wait for the candle to close above the resistance level or below the support level before taking any action."

# Action 51

| Date | Price | Action | Sign/ Candle |
|---|---|---|---|
| End Date D6 | P6 | P6<P5 | - /Red/Black Candle |
| D5 | P5 | P5<P4 | - /Red/Black Candle |
| D4 | P4 | P4>P3 | +/Green/White Candle |
| D3 | P3 | P3<P2 | - /Red/Black Candle |
| D2 | P2 | P2<P1 | - /Red/Black Candle |
| D1 | P1 | P1>P0 | +/Green/White Candle |
| Start Date D0 | P0 | | |

**The I Ching Says:**

**1a. Possible Plan of Action for the Day, Week, or Month After This Pattern Occurs:**

"Price swings may occur."

**1b. Check out these Sectors:**

Energy, Industrials, Real Estate, Technology, Telecommunication Services, Utilities.

**2. Likely Plan of Action for the Day Two, Week Two, or Month Two After This Pattern Occurs:**

There's a 50-50 chance that one of these two outcomes will happen:

"Exercise patience and wait."

**OR**

"Opting for a trending stock will enhance the chances of success."

# Action 52

| Date | Price | Action | Sign/ Candle |
|---|---|---|---|
| End Date D6 | P6 | P6>P5 | +/Green/White Candle |
| D5 | P5 | P5<P4 | - /Red/Black Candle |
| D4 | P4 | P4<P3 | - /Red/Black Candle |
| D3 | P3 | P3>P2 | +/Green/White Candle |
| D2 | P2 | P2<P1 | - /Red/Black Candle |
| D1 | P1 | P1<P0 | - /Red/Black Candle |
| Start Date D0 | P0 | | |

**The I Ching Says:**

**1a. Possible Plan of Action for the Day, Week, or Month After This Pattern Occurs:**

"Exercise patience and wait."

**1b. Check out these Sectors:**

Consumer Discretionary, Consumer Staples, Industrials, Materials, Real Estate.

**2. Likely Plan of Action for the Day Two, Week Two, or Month Two After This Pattern Occurs:**

There's a 50-50 chance that one of these two outcomes will happen:

"If your stock is above or below the 200-period moving average, near or crossing 52-week highs, or nearing 52-week lows, or if its support/resistance levels have been breached, then consider it."

## OR

"Expect a probable loss ahead."

# Action 53

| Date | Price | Action | Sign/ Candle |
|---|---|---|---|
| End Date D6 | P6 | P6>P5 | +/Green/White Candle |
| D5 | P5 | P5>P4 | +/Green/White Candle |
| D4 | P4 | P4<P3 | - /Red/Black Candle |
| D3 | P3 | P3>P2 | +/Green/White Candle |
| D2 | P2 | P2<P1 | - /Red/Black Candle |
| D1 | P1 | P1<P0 | - /Red/Black Candle |
| Start Date D0 | P0 | | |

**The I Ching Says:**

**1a. Possible Plan of Action for the Day, Week, or Month After This Pattern Occurs:**

"If your stock is from the Consumer Discretionary sector and is currently trending, there's a probable chance of success."

**1b. Check out these Sectors:**

Consumer Discretionary, Consumer Staples, Financial Services, Healthcare, Industrials,

Materials, Real Estate, Technology, Telecommunication Services, Utilities.

## 2. Likely Plan of Action for the Day Two, Week Two, or Month Two After This Pattern Occurs:

There's a 50-50 chance that one of these two outcomes will happen:

"Entering the market incorrectly carries a high probability of loss. Seek advice from a market professional."

### OR

"Expect initial losses but potential profits later."

# Action 54

| Date | Price | Action | Sign/ Candle |
|---|---|---|---|
| End Date D6 | P6 | P6<P5 | - /Red/Black Candle |
| D5 | P5 | P5<P4 | - /Red/Black Candle |
| D4 | P4 | P4>P3 | +/Green/White Candle |
| D3 | P3 | P3<P2 | - /Red/Black Candle |
| D2 | P2 | P2>P1 | +/Green/White Candle |
| D1 | P1 | P1>P0 | +/Green/White Candle |
| Start Date D0 | P0 | | |

**The I Ching Says:**

**1a. Possible Plan of Action for the Day, Week, or Month After This Pattern Occurs:**

"If your stock is from the Consumer Discretionary sector and is currently trending, there's a probable chance of loss."

**1b. Check out these Sectors:**

Consumer Discretionary, Energy, Financial Services, Healthcare, Industrials, Materials, Real Estate, Technology, Telecommunication Services.

**2. Likely Plan of Action for the Day Two, Week Two, or Month Two After This Pattern Occurs:**

There's a 50-50 chance that one of these two outcomes will happen:

"Small profits are possible with proper money management."

**OR**

"Expect probable stagnation or a downslide for this stock."

# Action 55

| Date | Price | Action | Sign/ Candle |
|---|---|---|---|
| End Date D6 | P6 | P6<P5 | - /Red/Black Candle |
| D5 | P5 | P5<P4 | - /Red/Black Candle |
| D4 | P4 | P4>P3 | +/Green/White Candle |
| D3 | P3 | P3>P2 | +/Green/White Candle |
| D2 | P2 | P2<P1 | - /Red/Black Candle |
| D1 | P1 | P1>P0 | +/Green/White Candle |
| Start Date D0 | P0 | | |

**The I Ching Says:**

**1a. Possible Plan of Action for the Day, Week, or Month After This Pattern Occurs:**

"If your stock is a large-cap stock from a trending sector, your trade is likely to be profitable."

**1b. Check out these Sectors:**

Consumer Discretionary, Consumer Staples, Energy, Financial Services, Healthcare, Industrials,

Materials, Real Estate, Technology, Telecommunication Services, Utilities.

## 2. Likely Plan of Action for the Day Two, Week Two, or Month Two After This Pattern Occurs:

There's a 50-50 chance that one of these two outcomes will happen:

"If a stock was previously in a consolidation phase and is now breaking through its resistance or support levels, there's a high probability of success."

### OR

"This stock is likely to go up. Seek advice from a market professional."

# Action 56

| Date | Price | Action | Sign/ Candle |
| --- | --- | --- | --- |
| End Date D6 | P6 | P6>P5 | +/Green/White Candle |
| D5 | P5 | P5<P4 | - /Red/Black Candle |
| D4 | P4 | P4>P3 | +/Green/White Candle |
| D3 | P3 | P3>P2 | +/Green/White Candle |
| D2 | P2 | P2<P1 | - /Red/Black Candle |
| D1 | P1 | P1<P0 | - /Red/Black Candle |
| Start Date D0 | P0 | | |

**The I Ching Says:**

**1a. Possible Plan of Action for the Day, Week, or Month After This Pattern Occurs:**

"Stocks with momentum may yield small profits."

**1b. Check out these Sectors:**

Consumer Discretionary, Consumer Staples, Financial Services, Healthcare, Industrials,

Materials, Real Estate, Technology, Telecommunication Services, Utilities

## 2. Likely Plan of Action for the Day Two, Week Two, or Month Two After This Pattern Occurs:

There's a 50-50 chance that one of these two outcomes will happen:

"You can achieve a small profit with proper money management in place."

**OR**

"Prepare for a loss."

## Action 57

| Date | Price | Action | Sign/ Candle |
|---|---|---|---|
| End Date D6 | P6 | P6>P5 | +/Green/White Candle |
| D5 | P5 | P5>P4 | +/Green/White Candle |
| D4 | P4 | P4<P3 | - /Red/Black Candle |
| D3 | P3 | P3>P2 | +/Green/White Candle |
| D2 | P2 | P2>P1 | +/Green/White Candle |
| D1 | P1 | P1<P0 | - /Red/Black Candle |
| Start Date D0 | P0 | | |

**The I Ching Says:**

**1a. Possible Plan of Action for the Day, Week, or Month After This Pattern Occurs:**

"You can achieve a small profit with proper money management in place."

**1b. Check out these Sectors:**

Consumer Discretionary, Consumer Staples, Industrials, Materials, Technology, Telecommunication Services.

## 2. Likely Plan of Action for the Day Two, Week Two, or Month Two After This Pattern Occurs:

There's a 50-50 chance that one of these two outcomes will happen:

"Consider stocks with high momentum and volatility. Having a well-defined plan with proper entry/exit targets and trailing stop loss can lead to profitability."

**OR**

"Expect probable success."

# Action 58

| Date | Price | Action | Sign/ Candle |
|---|---|---|---|
| End Date D6 | P6 | P6<P5 | - /Red/Black Candle |
| D5 | P5 | P5>P4 | +/Green/White Candle |
| D4 | P4 | P4>P3 | +/Green/White Candle |
| D3 | P3 | P3<P2 | - /Red/Black Candle |
| D2 | P2 | P2>P1 | +/Green/White Candle |
| D1 | P1 | P1>P0 | +/Green/White Candle |
| Start Date D0 | P0 | | |

**The I Ching Says:**

**1a. Possible Plan of Action for the Day, Week, or Month After This Pattern Occurs:**

"Expect probable success."

**1b. Check out these Sectors:**

Consumer Discretionary, Financial Services, Healthcare, Industrials, Materials, Telecommunication Services.

## 2. Likely Plan of Action for the Day Two, Week Two, or Month Two After This Pattern Occurs:

There's a 50-50 chance that one of these two outcomes will happen:

"If your stock is from a dividend-paying company in either the Consumer Discretionary or Consumer Staples sectors, whichever is trending, there's a probable chance of success."

### OR

"If your stock is a large-cap stock from a trending sector, your trade is likely to be profitable."

# Action 59

| Date | Price | Action | Sign/ Candle |
|---|---|---|---|
| End Date D6 | P6 | P6>P5 | +/Green/White Candle |
| D5 | P5 | P5>P4 | +/Green/White Candle |
| D4 | P4 | P4<P3 | - /Red/Black Candle |
| D3 | P3 | P3<P2 | - /Red/Black Candle |
| D2 | P2 | P2>P1 | +/Green/White Candle |
| D1 | P1 | P1<P0 | - /Red/Black Candle |
| Start Date D0 | P0 | | |

**The I Ching Says:**

**1a. Possible Plan of Action for the Day, Week, or Month After This Pattern Occurs:**

"If your stock is above or below the 200-period moving average, near or crossing 52-week highs, or nearing 52-week lows, or if its support/resistance levels have been breached, then consider it."

**1b. Check out these Sectors:**

Consumer Discretionary, Consumer Staples, Energy, Financial Services, Healthcare, Industrials, Materials, Technology, Telecommunication Services.

**2. Likely Plan of Action for the Day Two, Week Two, or Month Two After This Pattern Occurs:**

There's a 50-50 chance that one of these two outcomes will happen:

"Select a trending stock for a better chance of success."

**OR**

"Follow the prevailing trend to make a profit."

| Date | Price | Action | Sign/ Candle |
|---|---|---|---|
| End Date D6 | P6 | P6<P5 | - /Red/Black Candle |
| D5 | P5 | P5>P4 | +/Green/White Candle |
| D4 | P4 | P4<P3 | - /Red/Black Candle |
| D3 | P3 | P3<P2 | - /Red/Black Candle |
| D2 | P2 | P2>P1 | +/Green/White Candle |
| D1 | P1 | P1>P0 | +/Green/White Candle |
| Start Date D0 | P0 | | |

**The I Ching Says:**

**1a. Possible Plan of Action for the Day, Week, or Month After This Pattern Occurs:**

"Exercise patience and wait."

**1b. Check out these Sectors:**

Consumer Discretionary, Energy, Financial Services, Healthcare, Industrials, Materials, Telecommunication Services.

**2. Likely Plan of Action for the Day Two, Week Two, or Month Two After This Pattern Occurs:**

There's a 50-50 chance that one of these two outcomes will happen:

"Maintain patience and wait."

**OR**

"Price swings may occur."

# Action 61

| Date | Price | Action | Sign/ Candle |
| --- | --- | --- | --- |
| End Date D6 | P6 | P6>P5 | +/Green/White Candle |
| D5 | P5 | P5>P4 | +/Green/White Candle |
| D4 | P4 | P4<P3 | - /Red/Black Candle |
| D3 | P3 | P3<P2 | - /Red/Black Candle |
| D2 | P2 | P2>P1 | +/Green/White Candle |
| D1 | P1 | P1>P0 | +/Green/White Candle |
| Start Date D0 | P0 | | |

**The I Ching Says:**

**1a. Possible Plan of Action for the Day, Week, or Month After This Pattern Occurs:**

"If your stock is above or below the 200-period moving average, near or crossing 52-week highs, or nearing 52-week lows, or if its support/resistance levels have been breached, then consider it."

**1b. Check out these Sectors:**

Consumer Discretionary, Consumer Staples, Financial Services, Healthcare, Industrials, Materials, Technology, Telecommunication Services.

**2. Likely Plan of Action for the Day Two, Week Two, or Month Two After This Pattern Occurs:**

There's a 50-50 chance that one of these two outcomes will happen:

"Select a trending stock for a better chance of success."

**OR**

"Follow the prevailing trend to make a profit."

**Action 62**

| Date | Price | Action | Sign/ Candle |
|---|---|---|---|
| End Date D6 | P6 | P6<P5 | - /Red/Black Candle |
| D5 | P5 | P5<P4 | - /Red/Black Candle |
| D4 | P4 | P4>P3 | +/Green/White Candle |
| D3 | P3 | P3>P2 | +/Green/White Candle |
| D2 | P2 | P2<P1 | - /Red/Black Candle |
| D1 | P1 | P1<P0 | - /Red/Black Candle |
| Start Date D0 | P0 | | |

**The I Ching Says:**

**1a. Possible Plan of Action for the Day, Week, or Month After This Pattern Occurs:**

"If your stock is a small-cap stock from a trending sector, your trade is likely to be profitable. Avoid large caps."

**1b. Check out these Sectors:**

Energy, Industrials, Real Estate, Technology, Telecommunication Services, Utilities.

## 2. Likely Plan of Action for the Day Two, Week Two, or Month Two After This Pattern Occurs:

There's a 50-50 chance that one of these two outcomes will happen:

"If a stock was previously in a consolidation phase and is now breaking through its resistance or support levels, there's a high probability of success."

### OR

"This stock is likely to go up. Seek advice from a market professional."

# Action 63

| Date | Price | Action | Sign/ Candle |
|---|---|---|---|
| End Date D6 | P6 | P6<P5 | - /Red/Black Candle |
| D5 | P5 | P5>P4 | +/Green/White Candle |
| D4 | P4 | P4<P3 | - /Red/Black Candle |
| D3 | P3 | P3>P2 | +/Green/White Candle |
| D2 | P2 | P2<P1 | - /Red/Black Candle |
| D1 | P1 | P1>P0 | +/Green/White Candle |
| Start Date D0 | P0 | | |

**The I Ching Says:**

**1a. Possible Plan of Action for the Day, Week, or Month After This Pattern Occurs:**

"Profits can turn into losses if you are not careful."

**1b. Check out these Sectors:**

Consumer Discretionary, Consumer Staples, Energy, Financial Services, Healthcare, Industrials, Materials, Telecommunication Services, Utilities.

**2. Likely Plan of Action for the Day Two, Week Two, or Month Two After This Pattern Occurs:**

There's a 50-50 chance that one of these two outcomes will happen:

"Expect initial losses before making a profit if you trade in this stock."

**OR**

"Consider retreating if you have a position in this stock. If you possess great patience, then hold on."

# Action 64

| Date | Price | Action | Sign/ Candle |
|---|---|---|---|
| End Date D6 | P6 | P6>P5 | +/Green/White Candle |
| D5 | P5 | P5<P4 | - /Red/Black Candle |
| D4 | P4 | P4>P3 | +/Green/White Candle |
| D3 | P3 | P3<P2 | - /Red/Black Candle |
| D2 | P2 | P2>P1 | +/Green/White Candle |
| D1 | P1 | P1<P0 | - /Red/Black Candle |
| Start Date D0 | P0 | | |

**The I Ching Says:**

**1a. Possible Plan of Action for the Day, Week, or Month After This Pattern Occurs:**

"Expect initial losses before making a profit if you trade in this stock."

**1b. Check out these Sectors:**

Consumer Discretionary, Consumer Staples, Energy, Financial Services, Healthcare, Industrials,

Materials, Technology, Telecommunication
Services, Utilities.

## 2. Likely Plan of Action for the Day Two, Week Two, or Month Two After This Pattern Occurs:

There's a 50-50 chance that one of these two outcomes will happen:

"If your stock is from the Consumer Discretionary sector and is currently trending, there's a probable chance of success."

**OR**

"Profits can turn into losses if you are not careful."

## Thank You!

Hey there, awesome readers! I want to express my heartfelt gratitude for taking the time to dive into my book. If you found it captivating and enlightening, I would be absolutely thrilled if you could leave a review. Your review holds incredible power, as it not only helps other readers discover the same incredible benefits you've experienced but also enables me to fine-tune my writing to serve you and all my other cherished readers even better.

Oh, and here's a little favor to ask: Could you spread the word about my book to your friends and relatives? It would mean the world to me if they could also grab a copy and embark on this amazing money- making journey.

Once again, thank you from the bottom of my heart for your unwavering support. You're the reason I continue to pour my soul into the written word!